TOP **10**
LAS VEGAS

CONNIE EMERSON

DK

EYEWITNESS TRAVEL

Left **Bellagio** Center **The Forum Shops at Caesars** Right **The Venetian**

LONDON, NEW YORK,
MELBOURNE, MUNICH AND DELHI
www.dk.com

Produced by Blue Island Publishing, London
Printed and bound in China

First US Edition, 2002
14 15 16 17 10 9 8 7 6 5 4 3 2 1

Published in the United States
by DK Publishing, 345 Hudson Street,
New York, New York 10014

**Reprinted with revisions 2003, 2005,
2007, 2009, 2011, 2013, 2015**

**Copyright 2002, 2015 © Dorling
Kindersley Limited, London
A Penguin Random House Company**

ISSN 1479-344X
ISBN: 978 1 46542 678 9

Within each Top 10 list in this book, no
hierarchy of quality or popularity is implied.
All 10 are, in the editors' opinion, of roughly
equal merit.

MIX
Paper from
responsible sources
FSC™ C018179
www.fsc.org

Contents

Las Vegas Top 10

The information in this DK Eyewitness Top 10 Travel Guide is checked regularly.
Every effort has been made to ensure that this book is as up-to-date as possible at the time of
going to press. Some details, however, such as telephone numbers, opening hours, prices,
gallery hanging arrangements and travel information are liable to change. The publishers
cannot accept responsibility for any consequences arising from the use of this book, nor for
any material on third party websites, and cannot guarantee that any website address in this
book will be a suitable source of travel information. We value the views and suggestions of
our readers very highly. Please write to: Publisher, DK Eyewitness Travel Guides, Dorling
Kindersley, 80 Strand, London, WC2R 0RL, UK, or email: travelguides@dk.com.

Cover – front: **AWL Images**: Gavin Hellier main; **DK Images**: Greg Ward bl. Spine: **DK Images**: Rough Guides/
Greg Ward b. Back: **DK Images**: Demetrio Carrasco tr; Alan Keohane tl; Rough Guides/Greg Ward tc.

Left **Golden Nugget Casino** Center left *Jubilee!* Center right **Wedding chapel** Right **Legacy Golf**

Contents (side text)

Left **Fremont Street Experience** Right **Grand Canyon**

LAS VEGAS
TOP 10

LAS VEGAS TOP 10

Las Vegas Highlights

The Entertainment Capital of the World offers just about everything: the world's largest hotels; the brightest stars in show business; shops and restaurants that rival any on earth. It's true, too, that the lights are brighter in Las Vegas. Yet you don't have to go far from the glamour and glitter to find the natural beauty of lakes and the desert as well.

The Strip
The neon artery of gambling pulses with excitement. Imaginatively themed resorts make it a street that never sleeps *(see pp8–9)*.

Hoover Dam
An engineering marvel, the dam not only tamed the raging Colorado River but also created the enormous Lake Mead, providing myriad aquatic pursuits, just minutes from the Las Vegas city limits *(see pp10–11)*.

Bellagio
The hotel that upped the ante as far as Las Vegas luxury is concerned. It is well located, too *(see pp14–15)*.

Downtown Las Vegas
The heart of the city in its early days, Downtown Las Vegas experienced a rebirth in the late 1990s *(see pp12–13)*.

ant.

Las Vegas Top 10

The Venetian 6
The Italian Renaissance revisited. Minstrels and nobility stroll among the Venetian landmarks; gondoliers glide by *(see pp20–21)*.

Grand Canyon 5
The ultimate excursion from Las Vegas. Whether their trip is by airplane, bus, or automobile, most visitors say the experience is unforgettable *(see pp16–19)*.

Wynn Las Vegas 7
This opulent mega-resort is set in beautiful landscaped gardens *(see pp22–3)*.

Red Rock Canyon 8
Not far from the city lights, this site provides a welcome getaway from all the glitz *(see pp24–5)*.

The Forum Shops at Caesars 9
The glory that was Rome provides the backdrop for a choice of upscale shops and restaurants *(see pp26–7)*.

CityCenter 10
This "city-within-a-city" is the most expensive privately funded resort complex in the United States *(see pp28–9)*.

The Strip

Nowhere are the glitz and glitter of Las Vegas, or its ambivalence, so apparent as along the Strip. This 4-mile (6-km) long thoroughfare (actually a section of Las Vegas Boulevard) is the entertainment capital of the world and home to many of the largest hotels and casinos on the planet. The extravaganza of both its adult entertainment and family favorites makes Las Vegas a city of superlatives. The Strip is a master of reinvention and re-creation, constantly changing, surprising, and embracing new ways to impress visitors.

The Strip by day

You're on vacation – why *not* have doughnuts for breakfast?! Delicious Krispy Kreme doughnuts are on sale at Excalibur, at the entrance to TI, and in other Strip casinos.

To experience the excitement fully, get a hotel room with a view of the Strip. Best of all are The Venetian, TI, or Trump International Hotel – ask for a room facing south.

Put on your shopping shoes early to beat the crowds at stores along the Strip. Or else patronize the hotel shops, which stay open until late.

- Map M3–R2
- General information: Las Vegas Convention and Visitors Authority
- 3150 Paradise Road
- 702 892 0711 or 877 847 4858
- www.lasvegas.com

Top 10 Sights

1. The Strip by Day
2. The Strip by Night
3. Older Hotel-Casinos
4. Theme Casinos
5. The Six Megaresorts
6. Fashion Show
7. The Forum Shops at Caesars
8. Hole-in-the-Wall Businesses
9. Hawaiian Marketplace
10. Impersonators

The Strip by Day
Although daytime lacks the glitter of the night, the Strip starts coming to life from mid-morning, when the street and sidewalks become thronged with cars and pedestrians. The Strip has been designated an All-American Road and Scenic Byway as it is a tourist destination in itself.

The Strip by Night
After dark is when the Strip is meant to be seen: its miles of neon tubes, millions of twinkling, pulsing, flashing lights, vast fiber-optic signs, and, of course, thousands of people create an almost euphoric excitement.

Older Hotel-Casinos
Riviera and Bally's are among the few surviving hotel-casinos of the 1950s to 1970s. Their façades and landscaping are grand but not over-the-top, reflecting the postwar era. Room prices are relatively low and many have been renovated.

For more on the Strip See pp70–77

Theme Casinos

New York-New York (see p32), Treasure Island – also called TI (see p33), Monte Carlo, and Luxor (see p72) were all built in the 1990s. As their names suggest, they are designed around themes. New York-New York has the energy of Times Square and TI (right) stages performances in Sirens' Cove. Ancient Egypt is the theme of the Luxor.

Fashion Show

The Fashion Show mall (see p52) proudly upholds the Las Vegas maxim that "bigger is better." This upscale mega mall houses 250 luxury shops and restaurants, and no fewer than seven major department stores are anchors here.

The Forum Shops at Caesars

A Las Vegas must-see, The Forum Shops (see pp26–7, above) combine entertainment, dining, and shopping. Let your taste buds tingle on a burger while your eyes feast on scenes from ancient Rome.

Hole-in-the-Wall Businesses

Clinging to life between the skyscrapers are simple one-story buildings that house everything from snack shops to tour operators. They are plentiful on the north end of the Strip.

Hawaiian Marketplace

Located in the center of the Strip between Flamingo and Tropicana, this kitsch island-themed plaza encloses retail, dining, and entertainment areas.

Impersonators

Elvis lives – at least, his numerous reincarnations do. Elvis Presley and Marilyn Monroe impersonators, among others, are a routine sight on the Strip. They perform in nostalgia shows; some even perform marriage ceremonies. Keep your eyes open, though: some real celebrities live here too!

The Mob

As is vividly portrayed in the 1995 Robert de Niro movie Casino, organized crime and Las Vegas were natural bedfellows for several decades from the 1940s. Gangsters were drawn like magpies to the glittering coins piling up effortlessly in so many slot machines. Bugsy Siegel was the trailblazer with his Flamingo Hotel (see p30), while Midwest crime boss Moe Dalitz opened the Desert Inn in 1950. Learn about Las Vegas' connection to The Mob and organized crime at The Mob Museum (see p81).

The Six Megaresorts

Bellagio (see pp14–15), The Venetian (pp20–21, right), Wynn Las Vegas (pp22–3), Mandalay Bay (p32), CityCenter (pp28–9), and Paris (p33) have all opened since 1998. Once you are installed you won't have to venture out again: all your needs are catered for.

Hoover Dam

Before the construction of the Hoover Dam early last century, the mighty Colorado River frequently flooded countless acres of farmland in southern California and Mexico. A series of studies into how to tame the rampaging river led in 1928 to the Boulder Canyon Project Act and the subsequent construction of the dam. This colossus of concrete – a triumph of engineering – not only provides reliable water supplies, flood control, and electricity, but is also a huge tourist attraction, with nearly a million visitors a year.

The top of the dam

🅐 While driving through Boulder City, stock up on beverages and mouthwatering sandwiches at Capriotti's Sandwich Shop (1010 Nevada Highway) to have as a picnic later on a Lake Mead beach.

🅒 Take a cruise that does not include meals: it will be cheaper and give you more time to take in the surroundings.

Drive along the west shore of Lake Mead on highways 166 and 167, to access the Valley of Fire and Lost City Museum *(see p98)*.

• Map T2 • 30 miles (50 km) SE of Las Vegas
• Hoover Dam Visitors Center, Hwy 93, Hoover Dam, Boulder City, NV
• 702 494 2517
• Open 9am–6pm daily
• Tour reservations 866 730 9097 (toll free)
• www.usbr.gov/lc/hooverdam

Top 10 Sights

1. Pat Tillman–Mike O'Callaghan Memorial Bridge (Hoover Dam Bridge)
2. Hoover Dam Visitors Center
3. Powerplant and Dam Tours
4. Lake Mead
5. Black Canyon River Raft Trips
6. Lake Mead Cruises
7. Scuba Diving
8. Boulder City/ Hoover Dam Museum
9. Construction Workers' Houses
10. Commercial District, Boulder City

Pat Tillman–Mike O'Callaghan Memorial Bridge (Hoover Dam Bridge)
Get a bird's eye view of the dam from the Hoover Dam Bridge. The sight of 3.2 million cu yards (2.6 million cu m) of concrete, standing 727 ft (221 m) high, is truly awe-inspiring.

Hoover Dam Visitors Center
Audiovisual and theater presentations as well as multimedia exhibits explain the processes and perils involved in building this eighth wonder of the modern world. An overlook on top of the center provides an eagle-eye view of the dam, Lake Mead, the Hoover Dam Bridge, and the Black Canyon.

Powerplant and Dam Tours
Visitors can descend to the powerplant's fifth floor or explore tunnels in the dam itself.

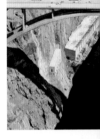

Transformers outside the powerplant

For more on the Hoover Dam and Lake Mead See pp92–7

Lake Mead
The dam's lake is the largest man-made body of water in the USA. Its 550 miles (885 km) of shoreline boast canyons and flower-rich meadows; its waters abound with fish. Boulder Beach offers the best swimming.

Lake Mead Cruises
The lake's shores come to colorful life from the deck of a boat *(left)*. You'll see sandy beaches and rocks of every hue. There's wildlife, too – look out for burros, jack rabbits, lizards, and the occasional bighorn sheep.

Scuba Diving
An unusual underwater scene greets divers: in addition to fish, there is a submerged factory where trainloads of gravel for the dam's concrete were cleaned and sorted. Take a trip with a local company; certified divers can rent scuba gear.

Construction Workers' Houses, Boulder City
Up to 8,000 dam workers were housed here, and although many of the buildings have disappeared, cottages 1–12 look much as they did when they were built.

Commercial District, Boulder City
Walk back into 1930s America. The arcaded, southwestern-style buildings were the precursors of today's shopping plazas. Boulder Dam Hotel, by contrast, is in Dutch colonial style.

Ancient Peoples
Archeologists disagree about how long humans have lived in the desert along the Colorado River. There were certainly people living downstream from the dam 3,000–4,000 years ago, and possibly as many as 8,000. The Patayans were among the first Native Americans known to live in the broader tri-state area (Nevada, Arizona, California), appearing in about AD 900; they lived in brush shelters and ate seeds and plants. Their descendants split into the Hualapai and Mojave tribes.

Black Canyon River Raft Trips
The Colorado River flows lazily below the dam, so rafting is pleasant rather than of the white-knuckle variety. It takes a little more than three hours to make the 12-mile (19-km) trip to Willow Beach. Look out for petroglyphs carved in the rock, and ringbolts: in the days before the dam these were used to winch steam boats through Ringbolt Rapids.

Boulder City/ Hoover Dam Museum
The dam and the people who built it are the focus of this museum, housed in the historic Boulder Dam Hotel *(see p93, above)*. Don't miss the film chronicling the dam's construction. Memorabilia, photos, and posters give insights into life in the 1930s.

For more outdoor activities **See pp60–1**

11

🔟 Downtown Las Vegas

During the 1980s and early 1990s, as the Strip became ever more glamorous, the downtown area – including the stretch along Fremont Street, formerly known as Glitter Gulch – went further and further into decline. City fathers and casino owners alike agreed that something had to be done to reverse the process and took action to see that it was. The resulting efforts have revitalized the area. Development is ongoing, with the opening of new restaurants and attractions offering a greater range of entertainment for visitors.

Fremont Street

🍴 For a memorable meal, try Florida Café Restaurante Cubano (1401 Las Vegas Boulevard S.).

🕐 Most of the action at night in downtown takes place near Fremont Street Experience.

Arrive a few minutes before the hour to see the light and sound show at the Fremont Street Experience. Then explore the shops and casinos or enjoy the stage entertainment until the next show begins.

• Map J–L4, L3
• Golden Gate, 1 Fremont St, 702 385 1906
• Golden Nugget, 129 Fremont St, 702 385 7111
• Binion's, 128 Fremont St, 702 382 1600
• Vegas Club, 18 Fremont St, 702 385 1664

Top 10 Sights

1. Neon Lights
2. Fremont Street Experience
3. Signs of the Past
4. Las Vegas's First Casino
5. Fremont Street Pedestrian Promenade
6. Golden Nugget
7. Binion's
8. Emergency Arts
9. Flightlinez at Fremont Street Experience
10. Entertainment

Neon Lights
The heart of downtown Las Vegas is home to the city's classic neon lights and signs. This is one of the brightest places on earth – so much so that you can stand on the street at midnight and read a newspaper. Even before the Fremont Street Experience was conceived, the country's leading neon designers and lighting engineers were strutting their stuff here.

Fremont Street Experience
Running from Main St to Fourth St, the Fremont Street Experience promenade's most prominent feature is Viva Vision, located near the Plaza Hotel-Casino. This is the world's largest graphic display system, and it contains 12.5 million LED lights, which provide incredible light and sound shows on the hour every hour from dusk until midnight. *(See also pp78–9.)*

Fremont Street Experience

Signs of the Past
Las Vegas Vic *(see p80)* has been waving to passersby on Fremont Street since 1951. More illuminating insights into the history of neon are at the Neon Museum *(see p45)* on the corner of Fremont and Las Vegas Blvd.

Las Vegas's First Casino
The place where it all started is the Sal Sagev Hotel on Fremont Street, which is now the Golden Gate. The strange-looking original name makes sense in mirror-writing. Today, it is famous not so much for gambling as for its shrimp cocktails.

Emergency Arts
Located in an old department store, this creative collective houses co-working space for artists and galleries, and an independent coffeehouse. There is also a yoga studio, hair salon, library, and even a ukelele club.

Flightlinez at Fremont Street Experience
For a great view, fly 750 ft (228 m) down the length of Fremont Street, suspended on a zip line 67 ft (20 m) above the promenade. Riders can reach speeds of up to 35 mph (56 kph).

Golden Nugget
The four-star Golden Nugget is the best-value hotel in the city (rates can fall as low as $60 in the off-season). Its casino is also first-rate (see p37). Try the Carson Street Café for its relaxing ambience – and also for some great people-watching.

Entertainment
In addition to the production shows and lounge acts at most of the hotels (see pp42–3), entertainment centers on Fremont Street. It's a popular venue for parades and performances by musical groups. (See also p82.)

Binion's
Dallas bootlegger and gambler Benny Binion established the property in 1951, and it was owned until 2004 by his descendants. The biggest names in poker continue to play at Binion's, although the World Series of Poker has moved to Rio (see p36). The hotel-casino is worth a visit to appreciate its old-time atmosphere.

Beginnings
For 20 years after its incorporation, entertainment in Las Vegas was limited to a few bars and brothels in the red-light district downtown. The legalization of gambling and arrival of 5,000 dam-construction workers in 1931 changed all that. Casinos opened on Fremont Street, and tourists began to arrive. World War II personnel and their families gave Las Vegas another population surge in the 1940s, and casino building continued apace after the war – as it does to this day.

Fremont Street Pedestrian Promenade
Pedestrians have direct access to 10 casinos and more than 60 restaurants from the promenade. Enjoy the vibe of open casinos, where the action spills out onto the streets.

For the top hotels and casinos in Las Vegas **See pp32–7**

TOP 10 Bellagio

From the flower arrangements in the halls to the fixtures in the bathtubs, Bellagio, built in 1998, is the epitome of extravagance. The goal of Steve Wynn, who originally conceived this grand monument to leisure, was to create a hotel "that would exemplify absolute quality while emphasizing romance and elegance – romance in the literary sense, a place of ideal beauty and comfort; the world everyone hopes for, as it might be if everything were just right." Most people agree that Wynn achieved his goal.

Façade of the Bellagio

For a leisurely lunch in a tranquil setting, reserve a table on the terrace at Olives, overlooking Lake Bellagio.

For a real treat, indulge yourself with an afternoon spent at the hotel's luxurious spa. Group booking can be arranged for brides and bridesmaids, and there's even a treatment menu specifically for men.

To enjoy the full effect of Bellagio's fountain show, cross the street and go to the observation level of the Eiffel Tower at Paris Las Vegas.

- Map Q1–2
- 3600 Las Vegas Blvd S.
- 888 987 6667
- www.bellagio. com
- $$$$$ (for price categories see p74)

Top 10 Features

1. Italianate Theme
2. Lobby Ceiling
3. Via Bellagio
4. Conservatory and Botanical Gardens
5. Casino
6. Gallery of Fine Art
7. Theater
8. Restaurants
9. Courtyard
10. Meeting and Business Facilities

Italianate Theme

Fronting on a pristine 8.5-acre (3.4 ha) lake with a tree-lined boulevard beyond, this extraordinary resort hotel was built to resemble an idyllic village on the shores of Italy's Lake Como. The Italianate theme is carried through the entire property – its original 3,000-room tower, the Spa Tower, 19 dining options, and two wedding chapels – creating an atmosphere of opulence. Building this representation of Italy cost $1.975 billion.

Lobby Ceiling

Visitors are greeted by a dazzling 2,000 sq ft (186 sq m) garden of glass flowers – the Fiore di Como – suspended from the lobby ceiling. The creator was Dale Chihuly, the first American artist to be designated a national treasure; amazingly, every single flower is different.

For more theme hotels See pp32–3

Via Bellagio
You are only likely to frequent Bellagio's shopping promenade if you have deep pockets. The establishments are as elegant as the Via itself, numbering among them such names as Prada, Tiffany & Co., Chanel, Giorgio Armani, Dior, Fendi, Gucci, and Yves St Laurent. *(See also p52.)*

Courtyard
With its Italianate columns and statuary, five outdoor pools, and four spas *(see p65)*, the formal courtyard at Bellagio is glorious for morning and evening strolls. During the middle part of the day, it is transformed into a scene of poolside cabanas, chaises (sunbeds), and umbrella tables, with bronzed sun-worshipers sipping cool drinks.

Casino
Aesthetically, this is the most pleasing casino in Las Vegas; it is less flamboyant and more sophisticated than the rest. Slot-machine carousels are fringed with specially designed fabrics rather than the ubiquitous neon tubing, and custom-made carpets provide a stylish relief from the norm.

Gallery of Fine Art
Bellagio's art gallery hosts major temporary exhibitions of important international artists, past and present, in conjunction with other large art galleries and museums in North America and around the world.

Theater
Designed for Cirque du Soleil's spectacular production "O" *(see p38)*, the theater combines old world magnificence (it is styled after the Paris Opera) with cutting-edge technology. Central to the production is a 1.5 million-gallon (6.8 million-liter) pool, which can be remodeled to meet each act's needs.

Meeting and Business Facilities
Bellagio has the capacity to host conference groups of up to 5,500 people in 50 different rooms, including three ballrooms. A professional staff is on hand to assist with needs such as word processing.

High Rollers
High rollers – gambling's big spenders – are courted by every major casino. Who qualifies (based on the amount he or she bets) varies a good deal, but a really big spender – someone who wagers thousands in an evening – will get superstar treatment from the top hotels. They may get flown to Las Vegas in a private jet, put up in a luxurious suite, and given carte blanche to order whatever they want from the hotel. Like superstars, high rollers are also treated with the ultimate discretion, so you may not spot one.

Conservatory and Botanical Gardens
Keen gardeners and plant-lovers will be rewarded with floral displays that change with each season and Chinese New Year. Each change employs the services of no fewer than 140 professionals.

Restaurants
Bellagio's superb restaurants include Le Cirque, Michael Mina, Noodles, Jasmine, and Yellowtail. Picasso *(see p46)* has an AAA Five Diamond Award and is decorated with originals.

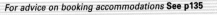

For advice on booking accommodations See p135

Grand Canyon

"Overwhelming" and "humbling" are words frequently used to describe the Grand Canyon experience. One of the world's most awesome sights, the canyon is 277 miles (443 km) long, 10 miles (16 km) wide, and as deep as a mile (1.6 km) in places. Because of the vast differences in elevation between floor and rim, the canyon encompasses a range of desert and mountain habitats. The South Rim, easier to access via road than the North Rim, is a five-hour drive away from Las Vegas.

Layers of the canyon wall

🍴 See p106 for great places to eat at the Grand Canyon.

🚗 The South Rim of the Grand Canyon is accessible by road year-round, but the North Rim facilities and road are closed from mid-Oct or Nov to mid-May.

You will need a permit to camp outside the official campsites within the national park. Apply in advance at the Backcountry Information Center.

• Map V2 • South Rim 271 miles (434 km), North Rim 255 miles (408 km) E of Las Vegas
• Grand Canyon Visitor Center, open 9am–5pm daily, longer hours in summer, 928 638 7888
• www.nps.gov/grca
• Admission charge to enter national park $25 per vehicle or $12 per pedestrian or cyclist

Top 10 Features

1. Flyovers
2. Flatwater Adventure
3. Visitor Centers
4. Hiking Trails
5. Overlooks
6. Whitewater Rafting
7. Grand Canyon Railway
8. Tusayan Museum and Ruin
9. California Condors
10. Golden Aspen

Flyovers
Airplane flights to the Grand Canyon rank among the most popular day trips from Las Vegas *(see p109)*.

Flatwater Adventure
If you want a taste of canyon rafting, sign up for a one-day flatwater rafting tour. The tours begin at the Glen Canyon Dam and travel 15 miles (24 km) downstream to Lee's Ferry, which is the entrance to Marble Canyon *(see p105)* and the beginning of the Grand Canyon itself. Along the way, near-vertical canyon walls rise high above the lake-like surface of the river.

Visitor Centers
Information centers at the North and South Rims of the canyon supply free maps as well as *The Guide*, which has general park information, *The Jr. Ranger Guide*, listing children's activities, and *The Accessibility Guide*, with information for disabled visitors. Exhibits and bookstores are located near the centers. Great observation points are near both centers as well. Ask about evening ranger programs if spending the night in the park.

For more on the canyon and places to stay **See pp98–109**

Hiking Trails
Ranking high with South Rim hikers are the South Kaibab, Bright Angel, and Rim trails *(see p108)*. Popular North Rim day hikes include those along the North Kaibab, Bright Angel Point, and Widforss trails. Don't attempt to hike to the canyon floor and back in one day: get an overnight permit.

Overlooks
Grand views may be found from many canyon overlooks. On the South Rim, Hermit Road hugs the rim west of Grand Canyon Village with nine overlooks. See great views of the Colorado River far below from Pima Point. Motorists can use Desert View Drive (Hwy 64) along the South Rim east of Grand Canyon Village with spectacular views from Grandview and Moran points, and you can almost see down to Utah from the top of the 70-ft (23-m) Watchtower. The North Rim is closed from mid-October to mid-May.

California Condors
Standing over 3 ft (1 m) tall and with a wingspan of about 9 ft (3 m), the rare California condor may be spotted flying over the South Canyon Rim in summer.

Golden Aspen
In the fall, the North Rim explodes in a brilliant yellow blaze, as thick stands of aspen trees turn a golden hue.

Exploration of the Canyon
In 1869, Major John Wesley Powell, a veteran of the American Civil War, led an exploration party along the Colorado River through the canyon. On August 28, three of the men left the group at the rim of Separation Canyon. They were killed by Native Americans. Ironically, it was the following day that Powell's expedition emerged safely from the gorge, completing the first exploration ever made of the Grand Canyon.

Whitewater Rafting
Dozens of companies, like Canyon Explorations *(see p109)*, offer white-water rafting trips along the Colorado on the canyon floor. Trips vary in length from 6 to 16 days.

Grand Canyon Railway
Four classes of service are offered on a vintage train journey from Williams to the Grand Canyon's South Rim. Vacation packages are also available.

Tusayan Museum and Ruin
Ruins of rock dwellings inhabited by ancestors of the Hopi Indians around AD 1200 are preserved between South Rim Village and the park's east entrance. On display at Tusayan Museum and Ruin are artifacts, re-created dwellings, and exhibits from contemporary local tribes, offering a fascinating insight into a different culture. The museum is open daily.

📖 The Venetian

Fashioned after Venice, Italy, The Venetian is a massive award-winning property. This all-suite resort is located at the heart of the Strip, making it an ideal base from which to explore the rest of Las Vegas Boulevard. The Grand Canal Shoppes, an indoor streetscape complete with gondolas and singing gondoliers, all set against the backdrop of St. Mark's Square, offers plentiful shopping, and the gaming rooms and lavish spa are also noteworthy. In addition, there are more than 30 fine dining restaurants and three theaters.

Arcade in the grounds of The Venetian

🍴 Splurge on a meal at Wolfgang Puck's Postrio Bar and Grill, once named by *Hotels* magazine as "one of the ten greatest restaurants in the world."

🕐 It is almost as much fun – and a lot less expensive – to watch the gondoliers from land as it is to actually ride in the gondolas.

If possible, visit The Venetian when there is a full moon and the crowds have thinned: by moonlight it is breathtaking.

• Map P2
• 3355 Las Vegas Blvd S.
• 702 414 1000 or 877 283 6423
• www.venetian.com
• $$$$$ suites only (for price categories see p74)

Top 10 Features

1. Architecture and Ambience
2. Grand Colonnade
3. Grand Canal
4. St. Mark's Square
5. The Grand Canal Shoppes at The Venetian
6. Restaurants
7. Madame Tussauds
8. Special Events
9. Canyon Ranch SpaClub
10. Casino

1 Architecture and Ambience

The grandeur of Venice meets Las Vegas glitz, and the results are surprisingly spectacular. True, the Grand Canal is only 1,200 ft (350 m) long as opposed to 2.5 miles (4 km), but any lack of authenticity is more than made up for by the festive Las Vegas ambience.

2 Grand Colonnade

Reproductions of frescoes framed in 24-karat gold adorn the domed and vaulted ceilings. Marble floors, Classical columns, costumed courtiers, and a giant overview of the real Venice all serve to transport the imagination.

3 Grand Canal

Push the boat out and hire The Venetian's very own Wedding Gondola (*left*) for your marriage ceremony! You can even sail under the Rialto Bridge.

 For more theme hotels **See pp32–3**

The Grand Canal Shoppes at The Venetian

The galaxy of goodies in the shops along the canal *(see p53; left)* satisfy a wide range of tastes: there are magic tricks at Houdini's and ice-cream at Haagen Dāzs; there is crystal at Swarovski and smart sportswear at Banana Republic. Travel by gondola or meander the long walkway linking the stores.

Restaurants

Stars of The Venetian's gastronomic line-up include celebrity restauranteur Wolfgang Puck's superb Postrio Bar and Grill, Mario Batali's B & B Ristorante, TAO Asian Bistro and Pierre Selvaggio's Valentino. Dine al fresco in St. Mark's Square to re-create the Venetian experience.

Madame Tussauds

In a building fashioned after the library on St. Mark's Square, the wax museum opened in 1999 and features well-known celebrities such as Frank Sinatra *(above)*. Some say the figures are even more lifelike than those in the London original *(see p44)*.

St. Mark's Square

So the geography isn't exactly as per the original, but even if you notice you probably won't care – the total effect is, aesthetically, extremely pleasing, perhaps more so than at any of the other resorts.

Special Events

Throughout the year, The Venetian hosts events, such as an annual tribute event honoring troops and wounded veterans, and dragon dances during Chinese New Year.

Canyon Ranch SpaClub

The largest of its kind in North America, The Venetian's spa has an indoor rock climbing wall, 2 fitness centers, and more than 80 treatment rooms.

Casino

Set in the Doge's Palace, the vast casino has 110 table games and 2,000 slot machines. On the walls of the high rollers' "Renaissance Room" hang works by Tiepolo, Tintoretto, and Titian. There is a 10,000 sq ft (929 sq m) race and sportsbook on the casino floor, with over 100 seats for personal betting stations.

High Hurdles

The journey of a major hotel-casino from the drawing board to the grand opening is a long and often tortuous process. Of course, plans must be submitted and approved by city government and county commissioners. But the most rigorous scrutiny is reserved not for the building but for those involved in owning and managing the casino. These people are vetted by the Nevada Gaming Commission and subjected to a thorough background check before a gaming license is issued.

 For more on museums **See pp44–5**

⏸0 Wynn Las Vegas

Built on the site of the legendary Desert Inn – once owned by billionaire Howard Hughes – this mega-resort was designed to captivate the highest of high-rollers and the biggest of the big spenders. Over-the-top opulence, from its extravagant villas to the automobiles in the Ferrari-Maserati showroom, reigns supreme. Wynn's sister hotel, Encore, is a luxurious addition to the resort, with its own selection of restaurants, suites, shops, and entertainment. The grounds, with an artificial mountain and lake, are spectacular, too.

Poolside cabana

🍽 The Buffet features everything from sushi to steak, and an all-you-can-eat buffet. There are 15 live cooking stations, and the atmosphere is garden-like with topiaries and pretty foliage. Prices vary depending on the time of visit.

⏱ Wear walking shoes if you want to explore the resort as there is a lot of ground to cover.

Moderately priced fare can be found at Wynn's casual dining outlets, including Drugstore Café, Terrace Pointe Café, and Zoozacrackers.

• Map N2
• 3131 Las Vegas Blvd S.
• 702 770 7100, 888 320 7123 (toll free)
• www.wynnlas vegas.com
• $$$$$ (for price categories see p74)

Top 10 Features

1 Casinos
2 Le Rêve – The Dream
3 Suites
4 Fine Dining
5 Golf Course
6 Tryst
7 The Wynn Esplanade
8 Wedding Salons
9 The Grounds
🔟 Spas

Casinos
Both the Encore and Wynn casinos seem more intimate than their size would indicate. The gambling stakes on the slot machines and table games are higher than at other casinos, and the casino bars are classy. The decor is lavish, and there's not a flashing light or neon sign in sight. Tile walkways provide natural light and views over the indoor oases.

Le Rêve – The Dream
This aquatic masterpiece *(below)* is the work of Franco Dragone, who also created shows for Cirque du Soleil. The abstract production features fabulous costumes, jaw-dropping gymnastics,

elegant synchronised swimming, and comedy. Shows take place in a theater in the Round at the Wynn, where the stage is surrounded by a pool. There are no restricted views, though sections A and B are known as the splash zones *(see p39).*

 For more theme hotels See pp32–3

Suites
The wall-to-wall, floor-to-ceiling windows of the 1,300-plus suites look out on the Strip, golf course, or mountains. All guest quarters are enormous and feature European linen, elegant furniture, DVD players, and flat-screen TVs in both living and bath areas.

Golf Course
Owner Steve Wynn and golfer Tom Fazio collaborated in re-designing this huge course by moving more than 800,000 cu ft (23,000 cu m) of desert sand, repositioning trees, and adding features including the high waterfall that players walk under to get from the 18th hole to the traditional-style clubhouse.

Tryst
One of the most sophisticated and impressive clubs in the city, Tryst contains a marble staircase and the requisite pole dancing stage. The club is decorated with red velvet walls, and features a 94-ft (28-m) waterfall, and a patio that wraps around a semicircular lagoon. Table service costs hundreds of dollars, but drinks can also be bought at the bar.

The Wynn Esplanade
Behind the glass and chrome façades of Cartier, Oscar de la Renta, Judith Leiber, Manolo Blahnik, and almost two dozen other upscale stores, lies temptation galore for visiting billionaires and gamblers. Window shoppers can admire the cars at the Ferrari-Maserati dealership nearby.

Fine Dining
Wynn's and Encore's restaurants have celebrity chefs preparing some of the city's tastiest dishes. SW, Wynn Las Vegas' signature steakhouse helmed by executive chef David Walzog, fuses classic steakhouse fare with innovative touches. Sinatra, at Encore, focuses on Italian favorites.

Wedding Salons
For visitors planning to marry here, there are two wedding chapels with private foyers and bridal rooms. The Lilac Salon seats 65 guests, while the Lavender Salon accommodates 120. The Primrose Court provides a romantic setting for outdoor weddings under a canopy of trees.

The Grounds
The resorts' beautiful surroundings bloom whatever the season. Mature trees, dazzling beds, and manicured bushes line exterior walkways *(above)*. Inside, atriums and mini-oases decorate public areas.

Spas
Hotel guests can indulge in a range of wraps, massages, and other treatments. Clients can enjoy them in one of the 45 tranquil treatment rooms *(below)*, or at the poolside cabana *(top left)*.

Steve Wynn
If any one man can be credited with shaping the Las Vegas Strip, it is Steve Wynn. The creative casino magnate opened the Mirage in 1989 and a new era began – one that impacted on gaming around the world. When Wynn unveiled the Bellagio nine years later, the gauntlet for hotel-casino excellence was thrown down and the mega-resort trend was born. He describes his latest creation, Wynn Las Vegas, as "the most expensive, the most complex, the most ambitious structure ever built in the world ..."

🔟 Red Rock Canyon

About 225 million years ago, everything at Red Rock Canyon was covered by an inland sea. The escarpment, formations, and caves were created after that sea evaporated and wind and rain began sculpting the land. This remarkable desert region lies just 24 miles (38 km) from the middle of the Strip by car. A conservation area since 1990, it is protected from the asphalt and grass of city expansion. The 13-mile (21-km) scenic drive that loops off Highway 159 provides a good overview, but the best way to explore this part of the Mojave Desert is on foot.

Desert lizard

🍴 Stop at one of the Einstein Bros Bagels eateries in Las Vegas for a picnic lunch to eat at the Willow Springs picnic area.

♿ Wheelchair users will find plenty of accessible sights to explore near the visitor center and Red Spring boardwalk.

You will need a permit if you want to camp overnight or go rock-climbing at Red Rock Canyon. Apply at the visitor center.

Take the usual precautions when visiting a desert area *(see p133)*.

• Map T2 • 24 miles (38 km) from mid-Strip
• Visitor Center, 1000 Scenic Drive, open 8am–4:30pm daily • 702 515 5350 • www.nv.blm.gov/redrockcanyon
• Admission charge $7 per vehicle • Campground $15 per night, per site

Top 10 Features

1. Red Rock Vista Overlook
2. Visitor Center
3. Hikes and Guided Walks
4. Endangered Desert Tortoises
5. Children's Discovery Trail
6. Petroglyphs and Pictographs
7. Thirteen-Mile Drive
8. Bookstore
9. Desert Whiptail Lizards
10. Tinajas

1 Red Rock Vista Overlook

The view from this overlook (about one mile past the Hwy 159 turnoff to the Canyon) is of the Red Rock escarpment itself, which rises a breathtaking 3,000 ft (1,000 m) from the valley floor. Time your trip to get here at either sunrise or sunset when the colors of this Aztec sandstone are at their sensational best.

2 Visitor Center

The visitor center *(below)* has area maps and staff on hand to answer questions. It contains both indoor and outdoor exhibits featuring geological, cultural, and natural history displays.

Red Rock Canyon

3 Hikes and Guided Walks

Of more than 30 miles (50 km) of hiking trails within the canyon, the most popular include those to Calico Tanks (featuring red sandstone) and Oak Creek. Guided walks focus on aspects of the environment such as native wild flowers and the area's geology.

 For more parks and preserves near Las Vegas See pp98–109

4 Endangered Desert Tortoises

Look out for brown-shelled tortoises, which, with their lifespan of up to 100 years, may outlive you. They dig burrows in the desert and spend at least 95 percent of their long lives below ground. Astonishingly, adult tortoises can survive for a year without water.

6 Petroglyphs and Pictographs

The area around Willow Springs contains some fascinating prehistoric rock carvings and paintings *(below)*. The exact meaning of many of the incised and painted symbols is not known, but because the area's early inhabitants were hunters and gatherers, it is believed that many symbolize the procuring of food.

9 Desert Whiptail Lizards

Common to the western United States, these small lizards have pointed snouts and forked tongues, which help them eat termites, spiders, scorpions, centipedes, and lizards. Recognize them by the four or five light stripes along the back, and yellow- or cream-colored belly with scattered dark spots.

10 Tinajas

Prevalent in the Calico Hills and at White Rock Spring, tinajas (or tanks) are naturally formed rock catchments for water. They serve as drinking basins for wildlife and are good places to head to for photo opportunities.

7 Thirteen-Mile Drive

The main scenic loop *(above)* is a one-way road taking in the Rainbow and Bridge mountains, and the Calico Hills. Designated stopping points for views are scattered along the way. Head for Willow Springs for picnic areas. Most of the hiking trails are accessible from car parks on the loop.

5 Children's Discovery Trail

At the visitor center, children can inquire about the Junior Explorer discovery book and other scheduled educational or interpretive events. Up near Willow Springs is the Children's Discovery Trail to Lost Creek. Less than a mile long, this fun round-trip highlights points of interest along the way. The cliffs above the trail are a good place to spot unique-looking bighorn sheep.

8 Bookstore

The visitor center bookstore covers the local flora, fauna, and geology. Excellent Southwest-themed novels for children and books on local geology, history, and culture are available for purchase.

Cycling Culture

Highway 159, which leads out of Las Vegas toward Red Rock Canyon, and the scenic loop are very popular with cyclists, especially on weekend mornings. Use caution when driving on this road. Visitors who want to ride can rent bikes at Las Vegas Cyclery (10575 Discovery Drive), McGhie's (4305 S. Fort Apache Road) and other businesses. Keep an eye out for desert creatures such as jack-rabbits and snakes that may dart out onto the road. Take plenty of water and sunscreen.

🔟 The Forum Shops at Caesars

"So many shops and so little time" is the complaint of most first-time visitors to The Forum Shops. Opals from Australia, an endangered species store, couturier clothes, and art galleries – there are over 160 stores in all. The common areas of the complex are open 24 hours a day, so the savvy travelers who want to window shop and get close-up looks at The Forum Shops' fountains and buildings will stroll its lanes in the wee hours of the morning.

The Cheesecake Factory

🍽 Have lunch at one of the restaurants with a sidewalk café, from where you can watch the passing parades.

🕐 Visit during the holiday season to admire the elaborate decorations.

Walking from the parking garage to the shops is a shorter trek than through the enormous casino.

If you're visiting with youngsters, arrive early in the morning to avoid the daily rush of shoppers.

• Map P1–2
• Caesars Palace, 3500 Las Vegas Blvd S.
• 800 634 6001
• Shops open 10am–11pm Mon–Thu, 10am–midnight Fri–Sun
• Dining reservations 702 731 7731
• www.caesars.com

Top 10 Shops and Sights

1. Spiral Escalator
2. Architecture
3. Sky Ceiling
4. Joe's Seafood, Prime Steak & Stone Crab
5. Upscale Fashion Shops
6. The Palm
7. Planet Hollywood
8. Wolfgang Puck's Spago
9. Aquarium
10. The Cheesecake Factory

Spiral Escalator

The Forum Shops is home to an impressive freestanding spiral escalator. At three stories high, it is the first of its kind in the United States. It was designed exclusively for The Forum Shops by Mitsubishi and added in 2004 after an expansion to the complex.

Architecture

An ancient Roman Forum streetscape is the inspiration behind the design. The Roman Great Hall is 160 ft (49 m) in diameter and 85 ft (26 m) high. Look for ornate fountains and classic statuary in the central piazzas, and the 50,000-gallon salt-water aquarium.

The Sky above the Forum

Sky Ceiling

The domed ceiling of The Forum Shops simulates a constantly changing sky. The morning sun shines; afternoon clouds float by; evening stars twinkle.

Joe's Seafood, Prime Steak & Stone Crab

Main courses include quality steaks seasoned with Joe's spices, but the main draw here is the Stone crab from the Gulf of Mexico, served with Joe's home-made mustard sauce.

For more on shopping See pp52–5 & 116

5 Upscale Fashion Shops

The shopping mall is bigger than ever after a 2008 expansion. Top designer brands including Fendi, Gucci, and Valentino, help this mall retain its self-proclaimed title as the "shopping wonder of the world."

6 The Palm

In a city full of big-ticket steakhouses, this national chain is a standout eatery. The Palm has been serving delicious prime and aged steaks in its festive atmosphere since 1993. The walls are lined with fun, colorful caricatures of celebrities and dignitaries, who have passed through the restaurant at one point or another. The staff consists of dutiful veteran servers, who maintain an excellent standard of hospitality. Moreover, the wine list is exceptionally lengthy.

7 Planet Hollywood

This enormous restaurant is crammed with Hollywood memorabilia. Framed movie posters, celebrity photographs, costumes worn in famous films, and movie props make this café – according to its advertisements – one of the largest repositories for movie mementos in the world. California-style cuisine features out-of-the-ordinary sandwiches, exotic salads, and mouth-watering signature burgers.

8 Wolfgang Puck's Spago

Spago was the first of the celebrity chef restaurants on the Vegas scene, starting the trend that is upstaging the city's traditionally famous buffets *(see pp48–9)* with upscale dining. Duck with roasted garlic polenta and other unusual combinations are among the rotating specials at this sophisticated dining spot. Spago *(below)* is one of six Wolfgang Puck fine dining establishments in Las Vegas.

9 Aquarium

This vast, 50,000-gallon (189,000-liter) saltwater aquarium is home to more than 100 species of ocean life. Highlights include sharks and rays; there are also individual and schooling fish, which are normally found around coral reefs. Visitors can watch qualified divers feed the fish daily at 1:15 and 5:15pm, and there is a behind-the-scenes tour available daily Monday through Friday at 3:15pm.

10 The Cheesecake Factory

With more than 200 items on the menu, The Cheesecake Factory has everything from hot spinach and cheese dip with tortilla chips, bruschetta, and Tex Mex eggrolls to triple chocolate brownie truffle cheesecake. Entrées include a teriyaki chicken that incorporates banana slices, pineapple, and brown sugar.

Commerce or Entertainment?

In most US cities, shopping is an end in itself: go to the mall, make purchases, return home. In Las Vegas, however, shopping has the added dimension of being coupled with entertainment. The Forum Shops and some of the other hotels, including Paris and The Venetian, have musicians, singers, mimes, and other performers strolling along the shopping arcades entertaining the crowds. It's all free and it adds to the glamour and excitement *(see also pp52–3)*.

For more on Caesars Palace See p32

CityCenter

Las Vegas's largest creation is CityCenter, a "city-within-a-city" designed to have everything all in one place. Located on 67 acres (27 ha) at the heart of the Strip, the complex is home to five distinct properties – ARIA Resort, Crystals at CityCenter, the Mandarin Oriental, the Vdara Hotel, and the residential Veer Towers. The area also encompasses a casino, luxury spas, and several art galleries, all of which are within walking distance of each other. At a cost of $8.5 billion, CityCenter is the most expensive privately funded project in the United States.

Aerial view of CityCenter

🍽 Begin your day with a breakfast panini and a coffee at World News Kaffee's The Cup, on the 1st floor of Crystals, next to the valet entrance.

🚋 A free tram links CityCenter to the Bellagio and Monte Carlo, taking just 3 minutes.

• 3740 Las Vegas Blvd S.
• Map Q1–2
• ARIA Resort, 3730 Las Vegas Blvd S., 866 359 7111, $$$$ (for price categories see p74)
• Crystals at CityCenter, 3720 Las Vegas Blvd S., 866 754 2489
• Zarkana, ARIA Resort, www.cirquedusoleil.com
• Wolfgang Puck Pizzeria & Cucina, Crystals, 702 238 1000, $$$$$
• Mandarin Oriental, 3752 Las Vegas Blvd S., 702 590 8888, $$$$
• Vdara Hotel, 2600 West Harmon Ave, 866 745 7111, $$$$

Top 10 Features

1. Casino
2. ARIA Resort
3. Crystals at CityCenter
4. Shows
5. Spas
6. Dining
7. Mandarin Oriental
8. Fine-Art Collection
9. Vdara Hotel
10. Architecture

Casino
In contrast to the artificial light of most casinos, the gaming floor of ARIA Resort's casino is bathed in natural light. It offers a variety of games and has exclusive salons providing high-limit slot machines and table games for high-end players.

ARIA Resort
The ARIA Resort *(below)* boasts 4,004 high-tech guestrooms and suites with views of the Vegas skyline and surrounding mountains. There are four outdoor pools with cabanas, while inside, the hotel boasts 16 restaurants, 10 bars, a spa, and a theater.

Crystals at CityCenter
Shopping, dining, and entertainment are all under one roof at this vast retail center *(above)*. Designer stores include Tom Ford, Paul Smith, and the largest Louis Vuitton outfit in North America. Various works of art, including a three-story, nest-like Tree House and ice and water sculptures, are dotted throughout.

Shows
4 CityCenter plays host to an exciting array of Cirque du Soleil shows, such as Zarkana, an acrobatic spectacle of a production that is exclusive to the ARIA Resort. These extravaganzas *(left)*, which have also previously included Viva Elvis, are sure to enrapture audiences of every age.

Fine-Art Collection
8 There are permanent displays of fine art throughout CityCenter. Artists such as Maya Lin, Jenny Holzer, Frank Stella, and Richard Long have created pieces ranging from sculptures and paintings to large-scale indoor and outdoor installations.

Vdara Hotel
9 This 57-story, all-suite hotel and spa *(above)* is connected to the Bellagio *(see pp14–15)* and the Aria via a pedestrian walkway. Suites boast state-of-the-art technology and full-service kitchens.

Architecture
10 Unique architectural features by eight of the world's foremost architects, including Cesar Pelli, abound at CityCenter. Among the highlights is Crystals' quartz-shaped metal-and-glass exterior by Studio Daniel Libeskind.

Spas
5 CityCenter spas include the ARIA, with a water garden; the Vdara, offering holistic treatments; and the Mandarin Oriental, where Eastern techniques are used.

Dining
6 Dining options here include nearly every type of cuisine, as well as restaurants from top chefs, such as the Wolfgang Puck Pizzeria & Cucina.

Mandarin Oriental
7 Winner of the Forbes Five-Star Award for hotel, spa, and restaurant, the Mandarin Oriental *(below)* is a 47-story, non-gaming hotel with 392 spacious rooms and suites, and 225 luxury condominium residences. Guests check in at the Sky Lobby on the 23rd floor, and there is a sky bridge connecting the hotel to Crystals at CityCenter.

Eco-friendly Site
CityCenter was built with sustainability in mind, and the project has been certified by the US Green Building Council. The Aria is one of the largest hotels in the world with Leadership in Energy and Environmental Design (LEED) status. Features include natural lighting, an on-site combined heat and power plant, and a large-scale recycling program.

Left **Mormon fort** Center **The Rat Pack** Right **MGM Grand**

Great Moments in Las Vegas Histo

1 1855: Mormons Establish a Trading Post

Inhabited for centuries by Native Americans and encountered by Spanish explorers in 1829, the Las Vegas area was only permanently settled in 1855 when a group of Mormons, led by Brigham Young, established a trading post here.

2 1931: Gambling Legalized in Nevada

The relaxed gaming laws passed in the Silver State in 1931 encouraged widespread participation *(above)*. In reality, betting and gambling were already widespread and, in some forms, legal.

3 1935: Boulder Dam Dedicated by Roosevelt

The greatest hydroelectric project of the 20th century, the Boulder (later Hoover) Dam was begun in 1931 and completed four years later, at a human cost of 96 lives. *(See pp10–11.)*

4 1940s: Air Conditioning and Irrigation Arrive

The ability to keep buildings cool and the greening brought about by irrigation made the Nevada desert far more attractive to developers. In 1941, Los Angeles hotelier Tom Hull bought land three miles south of downtown for $150 an acre and built the 100-room El Rancho motel – a new concept in accommodation.

5 Christmas Day, 1946: Bugsy Siegel Opens the Flamingo Hotel & Casino

A handful of hotels and motels followed El Rancho, but only when mobster Benjamin "Bugsy" Siegel built the Flamingo Hotel & Casino was the hitherto Wild West feel of the town replaced with the Miami Beach-style that was to become the hallmark of the Strip.

6 1960: The Rat Pack Comes to Town

The extravagant Flamingo was widely imitated in the 1950s, and entertainment was an important part of the new casinos' allure. Frank Sinatra performed at the Sands Hotel in 1960, with friends including John F. Kennedy in the audience. From then on, Vegas became a playground of the so-called Rat Pack (Sinatra, Sammy Davis, Jr., Dean Martin, Peter Lawford, Joey Bishop, *et al*).

7 1966: Howard Hughes Arrives

Hughes's Summa Corporation was a dominant player in the Nevada hotel/casino industry. Legend (which makes up much Las Vegas history) has it that the eccentric billionaire arrived in town one day by limousine and was whisked up to his suite at the Desert Inn, where he lived as a recluse for several years, with uncut fingernails and hair *(above)*.

1990s: The Era of the Theme Hotels Begins

In the 1970s and 1980s, the hotels became larger and more flamboyant. In 1991, the groundbreaking MGM Grand, Treasure Island, and pyramid-shaped Luxor launched the theme hotel in earnest.

1998: Bellagio Opens

Hotelier Steve Wynn set a new standard for Las Vegas hotels with the luxurious Bellagio *(see pp14–15)*. The former owner of the Mirage hotel group (sold to MGM in 2000) is acknowledged as the creative force behind the modern resort concept.

2009 Onwards: The New Generation of Resorts

Las Vegas is a dynamic, ever-evolving city. The near future will see the realization of mega-resort "cities." Developments such as CityCenter and the revitalization of downtown are expanding options for accommodation, dining, and entertainment.

The Bellagio

Famous Residents

1 Jerry Lewis
The comedian who famously teamed up with singer Dean Martin performed in Las Vegas for many years.

2 Howard Hughes
The eccentric billionaire used his inheritance to make still more money in the film and airline industries before becoming a force in gambling.

3 Liberace
Wladziu Valentino Liberace – aka Mr Show Business – opened at the Riviera in 1955 and never looked back.

4 Clara Bow
Silent-film star Clara Bow, who became known as the "It Girl," lived in Las Vegas with actor husband Rex Bell.

5 Wayne Newton
In 1957, 15-year-old entertainer Newton started at the Fremont; he is still frequently seen at events in the city.

6 André Agassi
Born in Las Vegas in 1970, Agassi rose to become one of the world's greatest (and most popular) tennis players.

7 Debbie Reynolds
The film star was also owner of a hotel-casino and museum of Hollywood memorabilia.

8 Robert Goulet
The actor/entertainer was a veteran of such hit Broadway musicals as *Carousel* and *The Man from La Mancha*.

9 Siegfried & Roy
These legendary German magicians are among the city's best-known residents.

10 Phyllis McGuire
The entertainer is fondly remembered as one third of the singing McGuire Sisters, whose hits included "Sincerely."

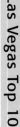

For the top casinos See pp36–7

Left **The Venetian** Center left **New York-New York** Center right **Caesars Palace** Right **Excalibur**

🔟 Theme Hotels

1 The Venetian
Whether or not The Venetian really evokes accurate images of Venice is beside the point: the sum of the hotel's parts adds up to an aesthetically pleasing whole (see pp20–21).

2 Caesars Palace
Caesars Palace opened in 1966 and was long the Strip's most opulent and, some would say, most ostentatious hotel. Times change, though, and Caesars has been forced to put millions of dollars into renovations in order to keep up with newcomers. Cleopatra's Barge – a floating lounge – is still as it was, and the cocktail goddesses still wear toga-like costumes, but new statues have been erected on the front lawn, and the former show theater, Circus Maximus, has been updated.
Ⓢ 3570 Las Vegas Blvd S. • Map P1–2
• 800 634 6001 • www.caesarspalace.
com • $$$$ (for price categories
see p74)

3 Luxor
One of the most distinctive buildings on the Strip, Luxor's 30-floor pyramid fronted by a giant sphinx sets the tone of this resort. Inside is a replica of the Great Temple of Ramses II and tiered stories that

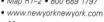

Hard Rock Hotel

lead to the top of the pyramid.
Ⓢ Luxor Hotel & Casino, 3900 Las Vegas Blvd S. • Map R1 • 702 262 4444
• www.luxor.com • $$

4 New York–New York
The Statue of Liberty raises her torch over the busiest intersection in Las Vegas. Nearby the Empire State, CBS, and Chrysler buildings rub shoulders with the Brooklyn Bridge, Grand Central Station, and the New York Public Library. Despite the architectural license, New York-New York is an exciting place with all manner of well-observed details.
Ⓢ 3790 Las Vegas Blvd S.
• Map R1–2 • 800 689 1797
• www.newyorknewyork.com
• $$

5 Hard Rock Hotel
The huge guitar sign outside and an enormous chandelier with saxophone pendants clearly identify this as a Hard Rock enterprise. Throughout the

Performance of The Sirens of TI

public rooms are displays of rock-and-roll memorabilia. And you'll hear only one kind of piped music, of course. ✪ *4455 Paradise Rd • Map Q3 • 702 693 5000 • www.hardrockhotel.com • $$$*

TI

This lavish hotel features a pool with private cabanas, gaming rooms, and an oversized hot tub for up to 25 people. Free nightly performances of *The Sirens of TI* are packed with daring swordplay, high-diving acrobatics, and pyrotechnics. Visitors can buy TI and Cirque du Soleil souvenirs in the shopping arcade. A pedestrian bridge connects the hotel with the Fashion Show *(see p52).* ✪ *3300 Las Vegas Blvd S. • Map P2 • 702 894 7111 • www.treasureisland. com • $$$*

Planet Hollywood

Vegas goes Holly-wood at this stunningly ultra-modern resort and casino conveniently located near the center of the Strip. The 2,600 movie-themed rooms will appeal to film fans, while the vibrant dining and nightlife options attract a trendy crowd. There is also a spa, two swimming pools, and 1,500-seat theater. ✪ *3667 Las Vegas Blvd S. • Map Q2 • 866 919 7472 • www.planethollywoodresort.com • $$$*

Paris Las Vegas

Alas, the City of Light has to lose something in translation to the City of Bright Lights. Even so, the Eiffel Tower model is impressive; the bicycle-riding delivery boy, and a cheery "bonjour" from valet-parking attendants are nice touches, too.

Paris Las Vegas

✪ *3655 Las Vegas Blvd S. • Map Q2 • 702 946 7000 • www.parislasvegas. com • $$$*

Circus Circus

As its name suggests, this hotel-casino contains the world's largest permanent circus, as well as an indoor, 5-acre (2-ha) theme park *(see p71).*

Circus Circus

Excalibur

One of the first theme hotels (built in 1990), this is still a favorite with children. The legend of King Arthur and his Knights is the theme that runs through the games arcade and on into the wedding chapel called the "Castle Walk." ✪ *3850 Las Vegas Blvd S. • Map R1–2 • 702 597 7777 • www.excalibur.com • $$*

Following pages **Caesars Palace and The Forum Shops**

Left **Rampart Casino** Center **Fiesta Rancho** Right **Harrah's Las Vegas**

🔟 Casinos

Rio All-Suite Hotel & Casino

1 Rio All-Suite Hotel & Casino
Cocktail waitresses in bright, flouncy costumes, an upbeat color theme, and friendly personnel make this casino a favorite with residents and visitors alike. The casino also has the reputation of serving the best food in town. Video poker is the most popular game here, perhaps because mini-TV sets are mounted on top of some of the machines. ⓢ *3700 W. Flamingo Rd • Map P1 • 888 396 2483 • www.riolasvegas.com*

2 Monte Carlo
The building reflects its European namesake, but the casino is typically Las Vegas, with the usual machines and table games. Monte Carlo's slot club is, however, superior to most; the air seems fresher than in most casinos, too. ⓢ *3770 Las Vegas Blvd S. • Map Q1–2 • 702 730 7777 • www.montecarlo.com*

Monte Carlo

3 Rampart Casino
This sophisticated casino provides a personable and intimate gaming experience. Highlights include a large selection of popular slot machines and knowledgeable dealers. ⓢ *221 N. Rampart Blvd • Map A3 • 702 869 7777 or 877 869 8777 • www.rampartcasino.com*

4 Santa Fe Station
People who suffer from claustrophobia in casinos will find relief here, where ceilings are high and small groups of machines are located near the entrance. An extensive remodeling program has added extra parking, state-of-the-art race- and sports-betting facilities, and more restaurants, including The Charcoal Room Steakhouse. ⓢ *4949 N. Rancho Drive • Map A1 • 800 678 2846 • www.stationcasinos.com*

5 Harrah's
One of the most respected names in the gaming industry, Caesars has more than a dozen properties across the USA and this one in particular offers value for money in service, food, and ambience. Harrah's has one of the best player's clubs as far as prizes are concerned; the club card can be used at any Caesars property around the country, so it works well for people who like to gamble wherever they vacation. ⓢ *3475 Las Vegas Blvd S. • Map P2 • 702 369 5000 • www.harrahs.com*

M Resort

Located 10 miles (16 km) south of the Strip, the M Resort sits at an elevation 400 ft (120 m) higher than any other Strip hotel-casino and boasts superb views of the valley. The stunning glass-framed hotel offers indoor and poolside gaming,

The Golden Nugget, Fremont Street

slot and video poker machines, a live action poker room, and a high-limit salon. ◎ 12300 Las Vegas Blvd S., Henderson • 702 797 1000 • www.themresort.com

Fiesta Rancho

The decor is unmemorable, but the slot and video-poker machines are considered the most liberal in town. There's a drive-up sports book – gamblers can place bets without getting out of their cars. Eateries are close to the casino floor, which is convenient for non-stop gamblers. ◎ 2400 N. Rancho Drive • Map B2 • 702 631 7000 • www.fiestarancholasvegas.com

Golden Nugget

This casino sets itself apart from its downtown neighbors, for both clientele and ambience. The restaurants are very good, and the casino is a pleasant place to gamble while waiting to see the Fremont Street Experience (see p79), which takes place just outside its doors. ◎ 129 E. Fremont St • Map K4 • 800 846 5336 • www.goldennugget.com

Sunset Station

Primarily patronized by local residents, Sunset Station is located across from the Galleria at Sunset shopping mall. The casino is light and well-ventilated. It also has a Kids' Quest (nursery) on the premises. ◎ 1301 W. Sunset Rd, Henderson • Map F6 • 702 547 7777 • www.sunsetstation.com

Sunset Station

ARIA Resort

This casino offers a high-tech gaming experience, with touch-screens displaying sports scores and restaurant menus, and interactive maps. There are several private gaming rooms too. ◎ 3730 Las Vegas Blvd S. • Map Q1–2 • 866 359 7111 • www.arialasvegas.com

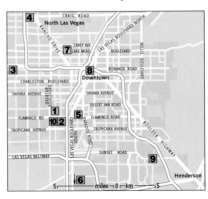

Left *Le Rêve – The Dream* Center *KÀ* Right *Blue Man Group*

🔟 Shows

1 "O"

"O," staged by Cirque du Soleil, is a circus quite unlike any other. The whole show revolves around the theme of water (hence the name, as in the French *eau*). The acrobats, synchronised swimmers, divers, and characters perform in, on, and above water. Seven hydraulic lifts raise and lower the water levels throughout the performance, allowing for spectacular diving and other feats.
🅂 Bellagio, 3600 Las Vegas Blvd S. • Map Q1–2 • 888 488 7111 for tickets

"O" by Cirque du Soleil

2 Mystère

Created especially for TI, *Mystère* is an enchanting circus that – like all Cirque du Soleil productions – has a mystical thread running through it. The costumes are innovative and colorful, and together with the high-energy acrobatics, evocative dances, and vivid lighting an overwhelming sensory experience is created.
🅂 TI, 3300 Las Vegas Blvd S. • Map P2 • 800 392 1999 or 702 894 7722 for tickets

3 Penn & Teller

Known as the "Bad Boys of Magic," for supposedly revealing the secrets of their tricks, Penn & Teller manage to break all of the rules of magic in this show. Edgy, provocative, and hilarious, on any given night the act can involve knives, guns, a fire-eating showgirl, or a duck. The show relies heavily on audience participation, with members invited onto the stage to take part in tricks. 🅂 Rio All-Suite Hotel & Casino, 3700 W. Flamingo Rd • Map P1 • 702 777 7776

Mystère, TI

4 KÀ

This innovative theatrical spectacle from Cirque du Soleil features astonishing acrobatic performances, martial arts, puppetry, multimedia, and pyrotechnics. The colorful and entertaining show was inspired by the Egyptian belief in the "kà," an invisible spiritual body which

Las Vegas Top 10

accompanies a person throughout their life. This theme is developed into an exciting tale about imperial twins who undertake a perilous journey into mystical lands. They face many challenges that must be overcome before they can fulfil their destiny. With astonishing computer-generated effects and 80 outstanding performers, the stage is brought to life in a blaze of fire and fantasy. ⊗ *MGM Grand, 3799 Las Vegas Blvd S.* • *Map R2* • *702 531 3826 or 866 740 7711 (toll free)* • *www.ka.com*

Le Rêve – The Dream
Le Rêve depicts a colorful world inhabited by beautiful, mystifying characters. Set around a 27-ft (8-m) pool, the show features breathtaking acrobatics, provocative choreography, and artistic athleticism. Live music and elaborate effects immerse the audience into a world of fantasy, adventure, and intrigue (see p22). ⊗ *Wynn Las Vegas, 3131 Las Vegas Blvd S.* • *Map N2* • *702 770 9966*

Jubilee!
Jubilee! features showgirls who not only look good but also dance well. The show offers an effective mix of production numbers and specialty acts, glamorous costumes, and pretty tunes. There are terrific special effects, too, such as the sinking of the *Titanic*. ⊗ *Bally's, 3645 Las Vegas Blvd S.* • *Map Q2* • *702 946 4567*

Blue Man Group
Unique, funny, wildly innovative, and with a contagious energy, this show is part-parade and part-dance party. Featuring comedy, drums, paint, and technology, it is popular with both children and adults alike. ⊗ *Monte Carlo, 3770 Las Vegas Blvd S.* • *Map Q1–2* • *800 258 3626*

Jubilee!, Bally's

The Beatles LOVE
Cirque du Soleil combines its magic with the exuberant spirit and timeless music of one of the most-loved bands in the world. ⊗ *The Mirage, 3400 Las Vegas Blvd S.* • *Map P1–2* • *702 792 7777 or 800 963 9634*

Absinthe
This adults-only show is a blend of carnival and spectacle, featuring wild and outlandish acts accompanied by outrageous humor in a theatre-in-the-round presentation. Audiences are awed by the acts performed mere feet away on an intimate stage. ⊗ *Caesars Palace, 3570 Las Vegas Blvd S.* • *Map P1–2* • *800 745 3000*

Mac King Comedy Magic Show
One of the funniest and most talented magicians in Las Vegas, Mac King keeps audiences alternatively spellbound and rolling in the aisles. His act includes rope tricks, a "Cloak of Invisibility," shadow puppets and goldfish. ⊗ *Harrah's, 3475 Las Vegas Blvd S.* • *Map P2* • *702 369 5222*

Left **Thomas & Mack Center** Center **Le Théâtre des Arts** Right **The Smith Center for the Performing Arts**

Music and Performing Arts Venues

1 Hollywood Theater and Grand Garden Arena

Headliners such as Tom Jones and David Copperfield, and music acts such as Sting and Aerosmith, regularly appear at the 630-seat Hollywood Theater *(below)*. MGM's larger 15,200-seat special-events center, the Garden Arena, is used for superstar concerts, major sporting events, and other spectaculars. It was the setting for the much-publicized Barbra Streisand Millennium Concert on New Year's Eve 1999, and has since hosted numerous high-profile concerts.
❧ *MGM Grand Hotel, 3799 Las Vegas Blvd S. • Map R2 • 800 646 7787*

2 Mandalay Bay Events Center

Luciano Pavarotti inaugurated the 12,000-seat events center in 1999. Since then, performers as diverse as tenor Andrea Bocelli (with the Russian Symphony Orchestra), Justin Timberlake and Kanye West have graced its stage. During one month in particular, the Mandalay Bay Center was exceptionally eclectic, staging as it did a heavyweight bout between Evander Holyfield and John Ruiz, skater Katarina Witt's *Kisses on Ice* show, and Bocelli's vocal performance.
❧ *Mandalay Bay, 3950 Las Vegas Blvd S. • Map R2 • 877 632 7800*

3 The Showroom at Planet Hollywood

The 1,500-seat theater at Planet Hollywood Resort & Casino *(see p33)* regularly draws renowned touring acts. The venue has hosted productions such as *Forever Swing*, the Broadway musical *Fosse*, and *Les Misérables*.
❧ *Planet Hollywood Resort & Casino, 3667 Las Vegas Blvd S. • Map Q2*

4 Sam Boyd Stadium

Built in 1971, the stadium hosts some of the biggest entertainment and sporting events in the country. Annual events include the Monster Jam World Finals and USA Sevens.
❧ *7000 E. Russell Rd • Map F5 • 702 895 3900*

5 The Smith Center for the Performing Arts

Featuring a 2,050-seat hall with brilliant acoustics, cabaret jazz stage, and intimate theater space, The Smith Center showcases full seasons of dance, music, and spoken word performances as well as Broadway shows. Take the time to visit Symphony Park in front of the hall and browse the artworks inside as well.
❧ *361 Symphony Park Ave • Map K3 • 702 749 2000*

For more on entertainment See pp118–19

Artemus W. Ham Concert Hall

Across the courtyard from the Judy Bayley Theatre, the Artemus W. Ham Concert Hall is an elegant building that serves as the venue for performances of both nationally and internationally acclaimed musicians and dancers. Violinist Itzhak Perlman and the Bolshoi Ballet are among the star names that have appeared here. ◈ *University of Nevada Las Vegas, S. Maryland Parkway* • *Map Q4* • *702-895-ARTS*

Thomas & Mack Center

Initially designed for college basketball, over the years the Thomas & Mack Center has become a site for major boxing matches as well as professional football and basketball tournaments. It has previously hosted the Vegoose Music Festival, and is one of the largest arenas in the city. In addition, the National Finals Rodeo is held here annually, drawing tens of thousands of fans. Family-style entertainment and concerts are just as popular as the sporting events. ◈ *University of Nevada Las Vegas, S. Maryland Parkway* • *Map Q4* • *702 895 2787*

Orleans Showroom

The 850-seat theater presents several headliners each month. The list of performers is a veritable "who's who" of the entertainment world of yesteryear: Jerry Lewis; Willie Nelson; Peter, Paul, and Mary; Roy Clark; the Righteous Brothers; and Crystal Gayle, to name but a few. ◈ *Orleans Hotel & Casino, 4500 W. Tropicana* • *Map B4* • *702 365 7111*

Le Théâtre des Arts

The Parisian-style theater opened in 1999 and has welcomed big names ever since, including Dennis Miller, Bobby Vinton, Earth, Wind, and Fire, and the Moody Blues. In 2008, it hosted the Broadway production of *The Producers*. ◈ *Paris Las Vegas, 3655 Las Vegas Blvd S.* • *Map Q2* • *877 374 7469*

Clark County Amphitheater

This outdoor amphitheater is the setting for a popular and eclectic range of entertainment, from the "Jazz in the Park" series and the Reggae in the Desert festival, plus various events that change from year to year. The amphitheater's "brown-bag"

Clark County Amphitheater emblem

lunches attract workers from nearby office buildings, Las Vegas residents, and visitors alike. ◈ *500 S. Grand Central Parkway* • *Map K3* • *702 455 8200* • *Events listed in local press*

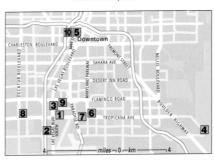

For free entertainment **See p76**

41

Left **TAO Nightclub** Center **eyecandy sound lounge** Right **Pure at Caesars**

Nightclubs and Lounges

1 TAO Nightclub
The original TAO, a celeb-filled Asian bistro in New York, gets a Vegas makeover at The Venetian (see pp20–21). Waterfalls, giant Buddha statues, and an artificial sandy beach are the major features of this Asian-themed club. On Saturday nights TAO's pool is transformed into an exotic nightspot, complete with a light show and floating Chinese lanterns in the pool. Famous guest DJs frequently spin tunes. Drink at one of the three bars or enjoy the magnificent views from the terrace. TAO is busy on weekends so reserve a table in advance. ⊗ *The Venetian, 3355 Las Vegas Blvd S. • Map P2 • 702 388 8588 • 10pm–5am Thu–Sat • Admission charge*

Ghostbar

Vanity

2 1 OAK
A favorite with celebrities, this 16,000-square-foot venue has two rooms, a top-of-the-line sound system, and 13 oil paintings by artist Roy Nachum. Designers of this nightclub have a superb eye for detail, and the service is considered one of the best in Las Vegas. ⊗ *The Mirage Hotel & Casino, 3400 Las Vegas Blvd S. • Map P1–2 • 702 588 5656 • Open 10:30pm–4am Tue, Fri & Sat • Admission charge*

3 Drai's
Book-lined Drai's is Las Vegas's only after-hours club. A fireplace, comfortable upholstered chairs, and potted palms add to the intimate atmosphere. With some of the world's greatest DJs playing everything from techno to Latin rhythms, the party usually goes on well after sunrise. ⊗ *3593 Las Vegas Blvd S. • Map P2 • 702 737 0555 • Open from 1am Thu–Sun*

4 LAVO Nightclub
This venue is small but popular. Elevated VIP seating, embossed leather walls, and mirrored mosaic tile niches are decor highlights. It is said to have one of the most energetic dance floors in Las Vegas. ⊗ *The Palazzo, 3325 Las Vegas Blvd S. • Map P2 • 702 791 1800 • Open 11pm–4am Sun, Tue & Wed, 10:30pm–4am Fri & Sat • Admission charge*

For more on live music **See pp40–41**

Tryst

eyecandy sound lounge

A unique and visually stunning bar in the center of Mandalay Bay's main casino. A kaleidoscope of colors enlivens everything from the curtains to the dance floor. ◈ *Mandalay Bay, 3950 Las Vegas Blvd S.* • *Map R1* • *702 632 7777* • *Open from 6pm daily*

Tryst

This hip nightclub is located in one of Las Vegas' mega resorts in the center of the Strip. Dress is casual chic, and definitely no hats, oversized jeans, or athletic wear allowed. Bottle service is required for reserved tables. ◈ *Wynn Las Vegas, 3131 Las Vegas Blvd S.* • *Map N2* • *702 770 3375* • *Open 10pm–4am Thu–Sat* • *Admission charge*

MARQUEE

This massive club has seven bars and three different rooms each with its own individual vibe – the Main Room, the Boombox, and The Library. An LED DJ booth dominates the Main Room. ◈ *The Cosmopolitan, 3708 Las Vegas Blvd S.* • *Map Q1* • *702 333 9000* • *Open from 10pm Mon, Thu–Sat* • *Admission charge*

Pure at Caesars

A three-level, mega-club owned by nightlife innovators Angel Management Group, it features an upscale VIP service and attracts some of the Strip's most stylish crowds. Opulent, oversized beds ring the main dance floor, while a huge outdoor terrace provides great views. ◈ *Caesars Palace, 3570 Las Vegas Blvd S.* • *Map P1* • *702 731 7873* • *Open 10pm–4am Tue, Thu–Sun*

Vanity

Antique mirrors and hand-cut crystals adorn the walls at this opulent nightclub. Plush velvets and deep satins are the fabrics of choice, and there are two marble bars, a sunken dance floor, and intimate VIP booths. ◈ *Hard Rock Hotel, 4455 Paradise Rd* • *Map Q3* • *702 693 5555* • *Opening hours vary* • *Admission charge*

Ghostbar at Palms

One of the city's most futuristic and stylish nightspots, Ghostbar is best known for its "ghost deck" with its unforgettable views some 55 floors above the hotel pool. Attracts a young crowd. ◈ *Palms Casino Resort, 4321 Flamingo Rd W.* • *Map B4* • *702 942 6832* • *Open from 8pm nightly* • *Admission charge*

Left **Madame Tussauds** Center **Las Vegas Natural History Museum** Right **Bellagio Gallery of Fine Art**

⏱10 Museums and Galleries

1 Bellagio Gallery of Fine Art

This world-class gallery presents temporary exhibitions of 19th- and 20th-century artworks and objects drawn from international collections. ◈ *Bellagio, 3600 Las Vegas Blvd S. • Map Q1–2 • 877 957 9777 • Open 10am–8pm daily • Admission charge • www.bellagio.com*

2 Madame Tussauds

Get up close to your favorite celebrity at this famous waxwork museum. For authenticity, many items of clothing and props are purchased at celebrity auctions. ◈ *The Venetian, 3377 Las Vegas Blvd S. • Map P2 • 702 862 7800 • Open 10am–9pm Sun–Thu, 10am–10pm Fri–Sat • Admission charge*

Elvis, Madame Tussauds

3 DISCOVERY Children's Museum

Located in Downtown Las Vegas, the DISCOVERY Children's Museum features three stories and 58,000 square feet (5388 sq m) of educational play for children and families. There are also 9 exhibition galleries and a 60-ft (18-m) summit climbing exhibit. ◈ *Donald W. Reynolds Discovery Center, 360 Promenade Place, Symphony Park • Map K3 • Admission charge • www.discovery kidslv.org*

4 Atomic Testing Museum

Nevada was the leading nuclear testing facility in the US from 1951 to 1992, and this museum tells the history of the Atomic Era with artifacts and re-creations from the Cold War period. The Ground Zero Theater is a bunker replica that shows visitors a film of an atomic explosion, accompanied by sounds, hot air, and vibrations. Las Vegas's weather station is located outside. ◈ *755 E Flamingo Rd • Map Q4 • 702 794 5151 • Open 10am–5pm Mon–Sat, noon–5pm Sun • Admission charge • www.national atomictestingmuseum.org*

The Marjorie Barrack Museum

For more children's activities See pp66–7

Nevada State Museum and Historical Society

This museum has a collection that includes specimens from Nevada mines, preserved Nevada wildlife, Las Vegas showgirl costumes, and a $25,000 chip from the Dunes Hotel. ✪ 309 S. Valley View Blvd, at the Springs Preserve • Map C3 • 702 486 5205 • Open 10am–6pm Thu–Mon • Admission charge

Neon Museum

Here, neon signs are seen as art. The museum offers a fascinating and eclectic collection of outdoor signage that casts an illuminating glow on Las Vegas history. The signs date from the 1930s to the present day. ✪ Map D2–3 • 702 387 6366 • Tours by appointment only – call to book • Admission charge • www.neonmuseum.org

Las Vegas Natural History Museum

Highlights include the international wildlife room, a children's hands-on exploration room, and a marine life gallery. The Treasures of Egypt exhibit features reproduced artifacts of ancient Egyptian life. ✪ 900 Las Vegas Blvd N. • Map J5 • 702 384 3466 • Open 9am–4pm daily • Admission charge • www.lvnhm.org

Clark County Heritage Museum

This unusual museum showcases historic buildings that have been relocated from sites around the state, as well as contemporary local artifacts. ✪ 1830 S. Boulder Hwy, Henderson • Map G6 • 702 455

7955 • Open 9am–4:30pm daily • Admission charge

Las Vegas Springs Preserve

The Springs Preserve explores Las Vegas's history through exhibits, botanical gardens, hiking trails, animal shows, galleries, classes and events for the whole family. ✪ 333 S. Valley View Blvd at US 95 • Map C3 • 702 822 7700 • 10am–6pm daily • Admission charge

Marjorie Barrick Museum

This museum has an extensive collection of contemporary and ethnographic art spanning 2,000 years and including crafts from Mesoamerica. The Xeriscape is an arboretum of drought-tolerant plants. ✪ UNLV Campus • Map Q4 • 702 895 3381 • Open 9am–5pm Mon–Fri, noon–5pm Sat • Free

Dinosaur, Natural History Museum

Left **Oscar's** Center **Joël Robuchon Restaurant** Right **Pamplemousse**

🔟 Gourmet Restaurants

Andre's

This restaurant *(above)* masterfully combines old-world charm with a modern twist. Signature dishes include rack of Colorado lamb with eggplant (aubergine), parmesan, and *gratin dauphinois* (potato in creamy cheese and garlic sauce). Service is gracious, and Andre Rochat presides over the kitchen. ◈ *Monte Carlo, 3770 Las Vegas Blvd S. • Map Q1–2 • 702 798 7151 • $$$$$ (for price categories see p90)*

Pamplemousse

With rough-hewn beams, baskets of fresh flowers on the tables, and nooks decorated with pottery and copper cookware, Pamplemousse ("grapefruit" in French) resembles a dining room in Provence. Dinner begins with a basket of fresh seasonal vegetables to create a custom salad. Entrées include veal medallions in a dijon-accented cream sauce, and roast duckling in a red wine and rum sauce. ◈ *400 E. Sahara Ave • Map M3 • 702 733 2066 • $$$$$*

Picasso

The room is exquisite, with original Picassos on the walls and a carpet designed by Pablo Picasso's son, Claude, underfoot. Spanish-born chef, Julian Serrano, creates contemporary French dishes with an Iberian accent. Among the delights are Maine lobster salad, pan-seared scallop, sautéed steak of foie gras, and sautéed filet of halibut. ◈ *Bellagio, 3600 Las Vegas Blvd S. • Map Q1–2 • 702 693 7223 • $$$$$*

Joël Robuchon Restaurant

A feast for both the palate and the eyes, the food at this outstanding restaurant is predominantly French with Asian and Spanish influences. Signature dishes include Le Caviar, a trio dish of thin couscous and Oscetra caviar, smooth cauliflower cream, and a delicate gelée of green asparagus. ◈ *MGM Grand, 3799 Las Vegas Blvd S. • Map R2 • 702 891 7925 • $$$$$*

Picasso

Oscar's

Located in the iconic dome of the Plaza Hotel-Casino, Oscar's Steakhouse features perfectly aged steaks, made-from-scratch sides, family-inspired recipes, and handcrafted cocktails. Oscar's has a retro-meets-modern decor with unique Vegas memorabilia from the restaurant's namesake, former Las Vegas Mayor Oscar Goodman. ✪ *Plaza Hotel-Casino, 1 Main St • Map J4 • 702 386 7227 • $$$$$*

Mastro's Ocean Club
This well-known nation-wide chain offers fresh seafood and pricey steaks. Small yet impressive, the restaurant is located at Crystals in CityCenter and has classic, sophisticated interiors. The views of the mall's incredible architectural creation, the Tree House, are stunning. ✪ *CityCenter, 3720 Las Vegas Blvd • Map Q1 • 702 798 7115 • $$$$$*

Prime Steakhouse
Superstar Chef Jean-Georges Vongerichten takes classic steak-house dining to new heights. Porterhouse with shishito peppers and caramelized brussels sprouts with maple-roasted quince is a signature dish. ✪ *Bellagio, 3600 Las Vegas Blvd S. • Map Q1 • 702 693 7111 • $$$$*

Mon Ami Gabi at Paris Las Vegas
Menu highlights at this Baroque-style, authentic Parisian bistro include the onion soup, steak frites, and strawberry crêpes. There are breathtaking views of the Strip when dining alfresco on the terrace. ✪ *Paris Las Vegas, 3655 Las Vegas Blvd S. • Map Q2 • 702 944 4224 • $$$*

Roy's
The menu at this award-winning restaurant features innovative Pacific Rim cuisine.

Prime Steakhouse

The predominantly seafood dishes include *wasabi* crab stuffed mushroom benedict, and fire-grilled yellow fin *ahi* (tuna). There is a children's menu too. ✪ *620 E. Flamingo Rd • 702 691 2053 • $$$$$*

Bouchon Bistro
Established by one of America's most renowned chefs, Thomas Keller, this eatery offers traditional French bistro fare with style. The food is cooked using top-quality ingredients, and a unique wine list is on offer for all. ✪ *The Venetian, 3355 Las Vegas Blvd • Map P2 • 702 414 6200 • $$$$$*

Left and center **All-you-can-eat buffet signs** Right **Carnival World Buffet**

Salad Bars, Buffets, and Brunches

Village Seafood Buffet
This buffet was an instant success when it opened in 1997 and continues to be a favorite with local residents. Lobster tail, shrimp, clams, and other seafood are flown in fresh daily and kept fresh in saltwater; the seafood Mongolian barbecue is especially good. ⊗ *Rio All-Suite Hotel & Casino, 3700 W. Flamingo Rd • Map P1 • 888 396 2483 • $$$*

Carnival World Buffet
Half the fun here is watching the chefs work as they interpret the flavors of Brazil, the East, Italy, Mexico, and the USA in a staggering 1,000-recipe repertoire. ⊗ *Rio All-Suite Hotel & Casino, 3700 W. Flamingo Rd • Map P1 • 888 396 2483 • $$*

Bacchanal Buffet
This show-stopping buffet at Caesars Palace offers more than 500 fresh dishes and about 15 chef's specials daily. With its chic, upscale interiors and contemporary food presentation, the Bacchanal Buffet is worth a visit for its enormous variety of food. Choose from the air, wood and water-themed sections of the dining rooms. Don't forget to try the fried chicken and waffles, as well as the red velvet pancakes. ⊗ *Caesars Palace, 3570 Las Vegas Blvd • Map P1 • 702 731 7928 • $$$$*

Bellagio Buffet
A large, sumptuous dining buffet offering more than 60 dishes, ranging from Chinese to Italian, and from Japanese to new American cuisine. Specialties include all the shrimps you can eat, wild duck breast, and roast venison. Save room for the decadent cheesecake or the heavenly chocolate-dipped strawberries. ⊗ *Bellagio, 3600 Las Vegas Blvd S. • Map Q1–2 • 888 987 6667 • $$$*

Sweet Tomatoes Salad Bar
The cool green and white interior plus extras like custom-made omelets and stuffed potato distinguish this salad bar from its rivals. The choice of dressings is extensive, and the ingredients are garden-fresh. The homemade chili is divine. ⊗ *375 N. Stephanie St • Map E6 • 702 933 1212 • $*

Sweet Tomatoes Salad Bar

Golden Nugget Buffet

Flavors Buffet
The Caesars group of hotel-casinos has a reputation for excellent food. Although the buffet offerings at the Flavors Buffet are not as unusual as those of some competitors, the standards of preparation and service are consistently high. Folks in the know go for the salads and extremely attractive desserts. ◎ Harrah's, 3475 Las Vegas Blvd S. • Map P2 • 702 693 6060 • $$

The Buffet at TI
This buffet features a selection of barbecue, pizza, grilled dishes, and Asian creations as well as a wide variety of sushi. There is also a bakery with several dessert options. ◎ TI, 3300 Las Vegas Blvd S. • Map P2 • 702 894 7111 • $$

Studio B Buffet
Integrating a top-notch restaurant with live action cooking, this buffet is unlike any other in Las Vegas. The 600-seat restaurant serves some of the best patisserie desserts, including the popular mini crème brûlée, and numerous chocolate souffles, cookies, and tarts. ◎ The M Resort, 2300 Las Vegas Blvd S., Henderson • Map P4 • 702 797 1000 • $$

Golden Nugget Buffet
There are around 60 buffet rooms in Las Vegas, and most could not be described as aesthetically lovely. The setting of the Nugget, however, is just that. The dishes are pretty tasty, too: don't miss the fresh carved turkey and old-fashioned bread pudding. ◎ Golden Nugget Hotel, 129 Fremont St • Map K4 • 702 385 7111 • $$

Le Village Buffet
An innovative blend of offerings at the Paris Las Vegas, including omelets, imported cheeses, bouillabaisse, wild mushroom bisque, lamb, venison, prime rib steak, and huge shrimp, all followed by a wealth of French-inspired desserts. ◎ Paris Las Vegas, 3655 Las Vegas Blvd S. • Map Q2 • 702 946 7000 • $$

For price categories **See p90**

Left **Little Church of the West** Center **Couple at Viva Las Vegas** Right **Touting for business**

🔟 Wedding Chapels

Bellagio Wedding Chapels
Bellagio's two chapels provide some of the most elegant and romantic wedding venues in Las Vegas. Both have a stained-glass window behind the altar, while ornate lamps and chandeliers of amethyst and Venetian glass complement the pastel shades of the furnishings. Personalized services are available for room reservations as well as both wedding and reception planning. ⑤ Bellagio, 3600 Las Vegas Blvd S. • Map Q1–2 • 702 693 7700, 888 987 3344

Viva Las Vegas
This chapel is known for its Elvis themed and traditional weddings as well as ceremonies set against backdrops such as the Red Rock Canyon. Stars like Angelina Jolie and Matt LeBlanc have made an appearance here. ⑤ 1205 Las Vegas Blvd S. • Map L3 • 702 384 0771

Little Church of the West
The Little Church opened in 1942, making it the oldest wedding chapel in town. It is a favorite with the stars: Zsa Zsa Gabor and George Saunders, Angelina Jolie and Billy Bob Thornton, and model Cindy Crawford and actor

Richard Gere have all graced its portals. ⑤ 4617 Las Vegas Blvd S. • Map C5 • 702 739 7971

Jewish Temples
Very few churches and synagogues – as distinct from wedding chapels – perform "walk-in" ceremonies. Marriage requirements vary from congregation to congregation. Contact Temple Beth Sholom for more information. ⑤ Temple Beth Sholom (Conservative United), 10700 Havenwood Ln • 702 804 1333

Christ Church Episcopal
This traditional Episcopal church is the closest one to the Strip. Bear in mind that churches in the Episcopal Diocese of Nevada require pre-nuptial meetings with the church's rector before a wedding can be performed. ⑤ 2000 S. Maryland Parkway • Map M4 • 702 735 7655

Wedding Salons at Wynn
Wynn Las Vegas has three wedding salons – two indoors and one outdoors. For couples

Wedding Salons at Wynn

hoping to ease the stress, seven wedding packages are available ranging from the simple to the over-the-top opulent. ◈ *Wynn Las Vegas, 3131 Las Vegas Blvd S.* • *Map N2* • *702 770 7400*

7 Canterbury Wedding Chapels

Create your own version of Camelot by marrying your knight in shining armor in one of Excalibur's two medieval-style chapels. For those seeking a truly historic wedding, don't be deterred if you don't have a ballgown or suit of armor; a variety of men's and women's costumes are available for rent. Vow-renewal services are also on offer for the already-wed. ◈ *Excalibur, 3850 Las Vegas Blvd S.* • *Map R1–2* • *702 597 7278*

8 Island Wedding Chapel

Located at the Tropicana, this chapel offers wedding ceremonies in a tropical paradise. The wedding chapel can accommodate the most guests, while the Island Arbor and Arbor Courtyard offer more intimate settings. Several packages are available, which cater to a variety of wedding dreams. ◈ *3801 Las Vegas Blvd S.* • *Map R2* • *702 739 2451 or 800 280 1187*

9 A Little White Wedding Chapel

This chapel represents what for many people is the epitome of Las Vegas; it has acquired a reputation for hosting rather unusual weddings. It was here in the spring of 2001 that a mass wedding took place, officiated by multiple Elvises. For the bride and groom who are acting on mad impulse or whose hectic lives leave them only a few minutes to spare, the Little White Wedding Chapel offers the world's only

A Little White Wedding Chapel

drive-up wedding window. The window never closes, and no appointment is necessary. ◈ *1301 Las Vegas Blvd S.* • *Map L4* • *702 382 5943* • *www.alittlewhitechapel.com*

10 Helicopter Ceremonies

For a wedding ceremony with a view, opt for A Little White Wedding Chapel's "Love is in the Air" package. It offers a limousine pickup, and the ceremony takes place during a scenic helicopter-ride over the Strip. ◈ *Little White Chapel in the Sky* • *702 382 5943*

Left **Canal Shoppes** Right **Fashion Show**

Places to Shop

The Forum Shops at Caesars

The Forum Shops are laid out along pseudo-Roman streets within the Caesars Palace complex, characterized by two-story storefronts topped with statues of Roman senators. Along with wares from Europe, American design is featured at stores like Banana Republic, Ann Taylor, and Brooks Brothers. During the holiday season, The Forum Shops are particularly popular. An expansion added a further 175,000 square feet (16,258 sq m) and additional levels to the complex. *(See also pp26–7.)*

Via Bellagio

Simply walking along Via Bellagio *(see also p15)* is an unforgettable experience. The boutiques are so opulent as to be intimidating: even if you dare not step inside, then at least the entrances to Fendi, Chanel, Gucci, and others are large enough to see inside. Tiffany's windows are especially dazzling during the holiday season. ◈ *Bellagio, 3600 Las Vegas Blvd S. • MapQ1–2*

Miracle Mile Shops

British fashion at French Connection, leisure wear at Urban Outfitters, and beautiful accessories at Swarovski are located here. In addition to 170 specialty shops, you will find Club Tattoo, featuring top tattoo artists. ◈ *Within Planet Hollywood Resort and Casino, 3667 Las Vegas Blvd S. • Map Q2*

Fashion Show

This upscale shoppers' paradise boasts Saks Fifth Avenue and Nordstrom department stores. The mall also hosts fashion shows and events. ◈ *3200 Las Vegas Blvd S. • Map N2*

The Galleria at Sunset

One of the city's residential malls, the Galleria at Sunset offers department store shopping and down-to-earth services, such as shoe and jewelry repair, free jewelry cleaning, alterations and tailoring, hairstyling, beauty treatments, gift wrapping, and postage stamps. ◈ *1300 W. Sunset Rd, Henderson • Map E5*

Via Bellagio

For more on shopping See pp54–5 & 116

Crystals at CityCenter
Featuring the highest concentration of designer flagship stores in the world, this high-end shopping area lures visitors with retailers including Prada, Gucci, Versace, Hermes, Valentino, Ermenegildo, Sisley, Jimmy Choo, Tiffany & Co., and Dolce & Gabbana.
Ⓢ 3720 Las Vegas Blvd S.
• Map Q1–2

The Grand Canal Shoppes at The Venetian
Located on the second floor of The Venetian (see pp20–21), the emphasis at Grand Canal Shoppes at The Venetian is on European elegance. Exquisite goods for sale include handmade Venetian lace, glass, and masks as well as silks, shoes, and jewelry from various European countries. Part of the pleasure of shopping at this mall is the distinctive ambience – it may not be quite like the real Venice, but the experience is enjoyable nonetheless.
Ⓢ The Venetian, 3355 Las Vegas Blvd S.
• Map P2

Mandalay Place
Mandalay Place is an eclectic selection of shops located on a 100,000-sq-ft (9,290-sq-m) sky bridge, connecting Mandalay Bay with Luxor Hotel and Casino. Stores include the world's first Nike Golf store and The Art of Music, which sells autographed memorabilia. There are plenty of restaurants and eateries as well, including Minus5, one of Las Vegas's ice bars. Ⓢ Mandalay Bay, 3950 Las Vegas Blvd S. • Map R1–2

Town Square Las Vegas
Take some time out from the Strip's sensory overload at this large outdoor shopping center with its village-like storefronts and quaint streetscapes. The 120-plus stores and restaurants include big-name favorites such as Abercrombie & Fitch, H&M, and Apple. There is plenty of entertainment with an 18-screen movie theater and a kids' playground, boasting a 42-ft (13-m) tall tree house and 30 pop-jet fountains. There are also several restaurants. Ⓢ 6605 Las Vegas Blvd S. • Map C5

Town Square Shopping Plaza

The Grand Canal Shoppes
The latest attraction for shoppers looking for luxury goods can be found within The Palazzo, which is connected to The Venetian. The Shoppes feature more than 60 high-end stores, such as the specialty fashion emporium, Barneys New York. Other fashion brands of note include Michael Kors, Christian Louboutin, and Diane Von Furstenberg. Ⓢ The Palazzo, 3325 Las Vegas Blvd S. • Map P2

Left **Dice clock** Center left **Circus Circus snow globe** Center right **Vegas puzzle** Right **Elvis glasses**

Souvenirs

1 Jigsaw Puzzles of the Strip
A pastime with no cash payout, but plenty of variety in terms of styles of puzzle and images of Vegas. The most popular are puzzles that piece together the Strip by night or form cartoon renditions of sights along the Strip. And since this part of Las Vegas is ever-changing, you may one day have a collector's item.

2 Personalized Poker Chips
The perfect souvenir for people who host their own card games. Personalized chips come in traditional colors (see p124), but can bear your name in place of a casino's name and logo.

3 Souvenir Photos
Have your picture taken dressed as a pioneer, a cowboy, or a showgirl. Or, if the fancy takes you, you can dress up in a medieval outfit. Alternatively, have your face substituted for a magazine-cover celebrity. The photos generally make fun mementos.

Retro slot machine

4 Elvis Sunglasses with Fake Sideburns
Although he didn't make much of a hit when he first appeared in Las Vegas in 1956, Elvis Presley has since been firmly associated with the Entertainment Capital of the World. Your career as an Elvis impersonator could start here, with a pair of these sunglasses and sideburns.

5 Dice-Decorated Clocks
Made of bright blue lucite, glittery gold plexiglass, brass, wood burls, or any other material known to man, these clocks – with dice marking the hours – fall into the genre of Las Vegas kitsch. Other tacky items include toilet seats inlaid with playing cards and poker chips, and tissue box covers with gaming motifs.

6 Books about Nevada
Las Vegas bookstores carry a large assortment of publications on the locale, including The Nevada Trivia Book by Richard Moreno, A Short History of Las Vegas by Myrick and Barbara Land, and several about slot machines by Marshall Fey (grandson of the inventor of the first slot machine). For fiction, try Sweet Promised Land or A Cup of Tea in Pamplona by the late Basque-American writer, Robert Laxalt.

7 Nevada-Made Gourmet Foods
The best-known Nevada-made edibles are Ethel M Chocolates, created by Forrest Mars Sr., a member of the Milky Way, Mars,

Poker chips

Three Musketeers, and M&Ms manufacturing family. For the more refined palate, try Mrs Auld's Sweet 'n' Spicy pickles, her scone mix, or brandied cherries; Davidson Teas are good, too.

8 Antique Slot Machines
Machines that date back to 1895 – when Charles Fey invented the very first slot machine, *The Liberty Bell* – occasionally appear on the auction block. Designs range from high Victoriana to Art Deco, and the rarer antique models can cost several thousand dollars.

9 Show Programs and Logo Items
Each major Las Vegas show has a shop associated with it, usually located near the box office. Commemorative T-shirts and various production recordings are the most common items for sale. However, anything that can be sold will be sold, including magicians' equipment, Chinese circus plates, and logo-emblazoned bottle stoppers, skipping ropes, and yo-yos.

10 Cash
The ultimate item to bring home from a Las Vegas trip has got to be several suitcases of hard cash. Although there are more losers than winners at the slot machines, roulette wheels, and gaming tables, visitors occasionally hit big jackpots, such as those on Megabucks and Quartermania machines, netting them huge sums of money.

Picture-Perfect Photo Spots

1 Bellagio Conservatory
Arrange your subjects in front of the most gorgeous floral display. The skylights give good light *(see p15)*.

2 Venetian Gondola
Professional photographers are available to capture your gondola ride *(see p20)*.

3 Hard Rock Hotel Swimming Pool
Best taken from a hotel room to get the pool's guitar shape *(see pp32–3)*.

4 Wynn Las Vegas Waterfall
Particularly beautiful once the sun sets and the water shimmers in the artificial light *(see p22)*.

5 Madame Tussauds
Have your loved one stand next to his or her favorite wax museum celebrity *(see p44)*.

6 Brahma Shrine, Caesars Palace
This lovely shrine is supposed to bring good luck *(see p32)*.

7 TI Gangway
Either of the ships makes a delightful backdrop for your photos, or take a shot of the ships and village *(see p33)*.

8 Downtown Las Vegas Entertainers
Pair your subject with a celebrity impersonator, who will be pleased to pose for a tip *(see p13)*.

9 Footbridge from Wynn to Fashion Show
A great vantage point for photographing the Strip. ⊗ Map P2

10 The Mirage Volcano
The massive volcano at The Mirage is a Las Vegas landmark and a spectacular free show *(see p73)*.

Left **The Big Apple Coaster** Right **Las Vegas Motor Speedway**

🔟 Thrill Rides and Simulators

1 The Big Apple Coaster

For those more thrill-seeking riders who dare to keep their eyes open during this white-knuckler, the Coney Island-style ride offers spectacular views of the Strip. The coaster route writhes, dips, dives, and loops around the resort's perimeter. While riding, you'll drop 144 ft (44 m) and hit speeds of 67 mph (108 kph). ⊗ *New York–New York, 3790 Las Vegas Blvd S. • Map R1–2*

2 Big Shot

Located on the world's tallest observation tower, the Big Shot shoots riders 160 ft (50 m) into the air. They then freefall back to the launch pad. It's not a ride for the faint-hearted, or for kids. Ride at night for a great view of the Strip. ⊗ *Stratosphere Tower, 2000 Las Vegas Blvd S. • Map L–M3*

3 The Desperado

Billed as one of the fastest roller coasters in the U.S., The Desperado reaches speeds of up to 80 mph (129 kph). Try to catch the great views of the Primm Valley from the highest point. If that isn't enough of a thrill, try falling 170 ft (52 m) on the Turbo Drop or get drenched on the Adventure Canyon Log Flume. ⊗ *Buffalo Bill's, 31900 Las Vegas Blvd S., Primm Valley, 35 miles (56 km) south of Las Vegas on I-5 • Map T2 • 702 386 7867 • Age, height, and weight restrictions*

4 Pole Position Raceway

This state-of-the-art race-kart facility offers a driving opportunity for beginners and experts alike. ⊗ *4175 South Arville • Map B4–5 • 7350 Prairie Falcon Rd • Map B2 • 702 227 7223 • Age, height, and weight restrictions*

Big Shot, Stratosphere

Canyon Blaster

5 There are some fun rides to sample at Adventuredome, Circus Circus' indoor theme park. Possibly the most exciting ride is the high-speed Canyon Blaster, which is billed as "the only double-loop, double-corkscrew indoor roller coaster." Disk-O is a dual rocking and spinning ride accompanied by loud disco music. Riders should expect plenty of twists and drops on the El Loco roller coaster. ◊ *Circus Circus, 2880 Las Vegas Blvd S. • Map M–N2*

Indoor skydiving at Vegas Indoor Skydiving

SkyJump Las Vegas

6 This "controlled free fall" lets brave souls jump 855 ft (261 m) from the 108th floor of the Stratosphere to a landing mat. Jumpers reach 40 mph (64 kph) as they soar through the air before landing with their feet back on the ground. Purchase a package deal to jump both at night and during the day. ◊ *Stratosphere Tower, 2000 Las Vegas Blvd S. • Map L–M3*

High Roller

7 One of the world's biggest ferris wheels, the High Roller stands at a height of 550 ft (168 m) and is located at the heart of the Strip. It provides fantastic views of the city from the top. ◊ *The Quad, 3535 Las Vegas Blvd S. • Map P2*

Airline Captain for a Day

8 Take control of a full motion flight simulator and feel what it's like to pilot a real Boeing 737. This 30-minute experience takes place in the same simulators in which real pilots train. ◊ *1771 Whitney Mesa Dr., Henderson • Map E5*

Vegas Indoor Skydiving

9 Vegas Indoor Skydiving advises potential customers that skydiving is not without risk, but this is a great place to gain wings without the use of an airplane or parachute. The one-hour experience includes training and a simulated skydive in a vertical wind tunnel complete with a mesh trampoline wall and foam-padded walls. ◊ *Vegas Indoor Skydiving, 200 Convention Center Drive • Map N3*

Richard Petty Driving Experience

10 After instruction, participants get into the driver's seat of an authentic NASCAR-style stock car, and go, go, go! ◊ *Las Vegas Motor Speedway, 7000 Las Vegas Blvd N. • Map E1*

For more activities for children **See pp66–7**

Left **Powerboat racing, Lake Mead** Right **National Finals Rodeo**

TOP 10 Festivals and Annual Events

1 Chinese New Year

Chinese New Year festivities center around Chinatown Plaza (see p85). Highlights include the traditional Chinese lion dance, firecrackers, foods, and *feng shui* as it pertains to the New Year.
◈ *Chinatown Plaza, Spring Mountain Rd • Map B4 • Late Jan–mid-Feb*

2 St. Patrick's Day Celebration

St. Patrick's parties are held at various restaurants and bars, with the main celebration at the Fremont Street Experience (see p79). Crowd-pleasers include a full line-up of music, entertainment on two stages, green beer (with green food coloring), and traditional Irish dishes.
◈ *Map K4 • Mar 17 or closest weekend*

3 Cinco de Mayo

The Mexican national holiday commemorating the victory of the Mexicans over the French in 1862 is celebrated up and down the Strip and around Las Vegas. Traditional Hispanic music is played in performance spaces, margaritas are poured freely, and typical food like tacos and *tamales* are served at celebration spots located around the city. ◈ *All around the city • May 5 or closest weekend*

Tournament golf

4 Snow Mountain Powwow

Tribal dancers in costumes decked out with beadwork, bones, shells, and bells come from across North America to perform ritual dances handed down from their ancestors. Feathered shields and foods such as Navajo tacos and fry bread are sold. ◈ *Paiute Indian Reservation, 30 miles N • May*

5 Greek Food Festival

For the past 37 years, the Las Vegas Greek Food Festival has celebrated all the aromas, sounds, tastes, and traditions of Greece. The festival runs for four days and includes continuous dancing with live Greek bands; fabulous Greek food; and stalls with gifts, jewelry, and art.
◈ *St. John the Baptist Greek Orthodox Church, 5300 South El Camino Las Vegas • Map B5 • 702 889 6376 • Sep*

6 Pacific Islands Festival

The many Pacific Rim peoples who live in the Las Vegas area celebrate their various heritages with traditional entertainment, cultural exhibits, and fashion boutiques. Food includes everything from *kimchi* and *poi* to potstickers and teriyaki. ◈ *Henderson Events Plaza, 200 S. Water St • Map G6 • 702 267 2171 • Sep*

7 Halloween Haunted Houses

Several companies have set up dozens of haunted houses in parking lots, community centers, and parks. Some are heavy on the scare factor while others are more like fun houses, with warped mirrors and twisted surprises. ◈ *Late Oct*

8 Vegas Uncork'd

Get a chance to meet celebrity chefs at this annual food and wine festival. Vegas Uncork'd offers a host of activities, from special tastings and wine dinners to seminars and interactive events. The activities are scattered around hotels such as the Bellagio, MGM Grand, The Venetian, and Caesars Palace.

9 National Finals Parties and BBQ Cook-Off

During the National Finals Rodeo, all of Las Vegas seems to go country – wearing jeans and boots. Casinos bring in country music bands, and line-dancing is encouraged. The free entertainment magazines are the best sources of information about what's going on where. The Cowboy Christmas Gift Show is one of the most popular events. ◈ *Various venues • Dec*

10 Magical Forest

Opportunity Village, an organization that helps the mentally challenged, raises funds by creating a Magical Forest with hundreds of decorated Christmas trees. Millions of holiday lights and a gingerbread house display are highlights. Nightly entertainment appropriate for all ages, and a fun passenger train make this a good family choice. ◈ *Opportunity Village, 6300 W. Oakey Blvd • Map B3 • 702 259 3741 • Nov–Jan*

Sporting Events

1 National Finals Rodeo

Cowboys compete for million-dollar prizes at the USA's premier rodeo. ◈ *Thomas & Mack Center • early Dec*

2 World Championship Boxing

Las Vegas is now the premier city for title bouts. ◈ *Caesars Palace, MGM Grand, Mandalay Bay, Thomas & Mack Center*

3 NASCAR Sprint Cup Series

Watch Sprint Cup car practices and races. ◈ *Las Vegas Motor Speedway • Mar*

4 Baseball

Watch the Las Vegas 51s on their home ground. ◈ *Cashman Field, 850 Las Vegas Blvd N. • Apr–Labor Day*

5 UNLV Sports Events

The university's Runnin' Rebels basketball, football, and baseball teams are hometown favorites. ◈ *Thomas & Mack Center, Sam Bowd Stadium, UNLV campus • Sep–May*

6 NHRA Summit Nationals

Dragsters battle for supremacy. ◈ *Las Vegas Motor Speedway, 7000 Las Vegas Blvd N. • Dates vary*

7 World Series of Poker

Poker players compete for $1 million. ◈ *Rio All-Suites Hotel & Casino • May–Jul*

8 PBR Championship

Professional bull-riding competition. ◈ *Thomas & Mack Center • Oct*

9 Las Vegas Triathlon

Sprint, Olympic, and half races. ◈ *Lake Mead • Sep*

10 Shriners Hospitals for Children Open

Attracts PGA golfers for a good cause. ◈ *TPC Summerlin • Oct*

Left **Jet skiing** Right **Cycling at Desert Shores**

🔟 Outdoor Activities

1 Hiking at Red Rock Canyon
Go south on 1-15, take exit 34 for 215 west, take exit 26 for Charleston Blvd, and head west to find the other-worldly Red Rock Canyon National Conservation Area *(above)*. A scenic drive loops through Red Rock Canyon: venture off this to get away from civilization. *(See pp24–5.)*

2 Cycling at Desert Shores
Cycling in Las Vegas can be pleasant – especially in the quieter, smarter residential areas of Green Valley and off Charleston Boulevard. Even better, though, are the paths at Desert Shores, in northwest Las Vegas, where you'll enjoy abundant shade and water views.

3 Water Sports on Lake Mead
Water babies should head for Calville Bay Marina, Las Vegas Boat Harbor, or Lake Mead Marina to rent jet skis, houseboats, water skis, and other personal water craft. Note that the wearing of life jackets is obligatory on personal water-craft. *(See pp92–5).*

4 Inline Skating in Summerlin
Summerlin is a planned community located northwest of downtown, and its smooth sidewalks are perfect for inline skating. The surroundings are among the most pleasant in the city, generally smog-free with attractive houses and condominiums. Experienced skaters may want to visit one of the city's many outdoor skate parks.

5 Tennis in Public Parks
Many of Las Vegas' public parks, including Sunset Park *(below)*, have plentiful well-lit tennis courts that are available

For more on hiking **See p108**

for general use. Visitors need to provide their own equipment. ◎ *Map D5* • *702 455 8200*

Skiing and Snowboarding at Mt. Charleston

Ball games in Sunset Park

Cozy in size, the Las Vegas Ski & Snowboard Resort offers light, dry powder snow with mostly sunny conditions. Lifts are typically open from November to April, with temperatures in the region of 86°F (30°C). Amenities, lessons, and rentals are available. The resort is located north of Mt Charleston off Hwy 156. ◎ *45 miles (72 km) NW of Las Vegas* • *702 385 2754* • *www.skilasvegas.com*

Disc Golf at Mountain Crest Park

This 18-hole course is both challenging and popular with locals, and it can be crowded on weekends, so let people play through to keep the game moving. Though the flow of the course works well, some tees are hard to locate, so ask other players if needed. You'll need to provide your own equipment. ◎ *4701 N Durango Blvd*

Outdoor Basketball

There always seem to be pick-up basketball games in progress at the public parks in Las Vegas. Most have several courts, many of which are in good condition. ◎ *Desert Breeze Park, 8275 Spring Mountain Rd* • *Sunset Park* • *Map D5*

Strolling the Strip

Although there are dozens of paths off the beaten track, especially in Henderson, most Las Vegas visitors do their strolling along the world-famous Strip. And why not? This road, actually a 4-mile (6.5-km) section of Las Vegas Boulevard South (or Hwy 604) is one of the most fascinating highways in the world. Comfortable shoes are a must, and carry water with you. Be safe in obeying traffic laws. ◎ *Map M3–R2*

Jogging at Sunset Park

If you're up to more than just a casual stroll down the Strip, one of the most popular joggers' venues is Sunset Park. Paths are well maintained and the circuit includes a fitness course. And there's plenty to look at to keep your mind off your feet: baseball, soccer, volleyball, and a popular playground near the park's lake. ◎ *Map D5*

For activities for children See pp66–7

Left **Las Vegas National Golf Club** Right **Angel Park Golf Club**

🔟 Golf Courses

1 Badlands Golf Club

Designed by golfers Johnny Miller and Chi Chi Rodríguez, this 27-hole facility weaves through deep canyons and offers true desert golf in a rugged setting. Four sets of tees make the course playable for everyone, from beginners to pros, and provide players with a wide variety of shot-making challenges. Stay & Play packages make planning a vacation easier. ⌖ *9119 Alta Dr • 702 363 0754*

2 The Legacy Golf Course

Designed by Arthur Hills, this course, which is popular with convention delegates, combines Scottish links-style golf with the dramatic desert vegetation of Nevada *(below)*. The course stretches 7,233 yards from the professional tees. The course highlight is the Devil's Triangle (holes 11–13). ⌖ *130 Par Excellence Drive, Henderson • Map E6 • 702 897 2187*

3 DragonRidge Golf Club

With its manicured fairways, bent-grass greens, and dramatic elevation changes, DragonRidge offers some of the most spectacular views in the valley. The course is private, with limited public play. ⌖ *552 S. Stephanie St, Henderson • Map E6 • 702 614 4444*

4 Bali Hai Golf Club

Just steps away from Mandalay Bay and Four Seasons, the course features thick stands of palm trees, large water hazards, tropical plants, and flowers in its South Seas design *(above)*. ⌖ *5160 Las Vegas Blvd S. • Map C5 • 702 597 2400*

5 Angel Park Golf Club

The Palm and the Mountain, this club's two 18-hole championship layouts designed by legendary American golfer Arnold Palmer, have been described as the "world's most complete golf experience." A night-lighted driving range, 9-hole putting course, and golf school form part of the complex. ⌖ *100 S. Rampart Blvd • Map A3 • 702 254 4653*

Angel Park Golf Club

6 Las Vegas Paiute Golf Resort
Set to the rugged desert land-scape, this was the first master-planned multicourse golf resort on Native American land. There are three courses, and the Snow and Sun Mountain courses were designed by Pete Dye, who has designed many esteemed courses. ⊘ *Snow Mountain, Highway 95 (exit 95), 20 miles (32 km) N of Las Vegas* • *702 658 1400*

7 Desert Willow Golf Course
This challenging course is carved from the foothills of the Black Mountains and surrounded by hazards and hilly terrain. This 18-hole, 60-par course is 3,811 yards long. ⊘ *2020 W. Horizon Ridge Parkway, Henderson* • *702 263 4653*

8 Las Vegas National Golf Club
Established in 1961, Tiger Woods played at this golf course on the path to his first PGA (Professional Golf Association) victory in 1996. Soft spikes are required on this course. ⊘ *1911 E. Desert Inn Rd* • *Map D4* • *702 734 1796*

9 Royal Links Golf Club
The course features holes inspired by famous holes on the Open courses in Great Britain. All the golf carts are equipped with GPS (Global Positioning Systems). ⊘ *5995 E. Valley View Dr* • *Map E4* • *888 427 6678*

10 The Revere at Anthem
Winding through three desert canyons, this course features natural changes in elevation and spectacular views of the Las Vegas skyline. The summer rates, as at many Las Vegas courses, are considerably lower than those charged at other times of the year. ⊘ *2600 Hampton Rd, Henderson* • *702 259 4653*

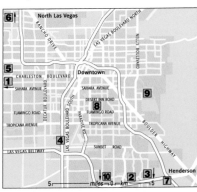

For more outdoor activities **See pp60–61**

Left **Stone massage** Right **Qua Baths & Spa at Caesars Palace**

🔟 Spas and Health Clubs

1 Canyon Ranch SpaClub

Residents at The Venetian can enjoy the 100-plus spa services, including movement therapy and 20 different styles of massage. The huge facility is also open to non-residents, as is the Canyon Ranch café. There is a full-service salon and an expansive co-ed lounging area. ◈ *The Venetian, 3355 Las Vegas Blvd S. • Map P2 • 702 414 3600*

2 Aquae Sulis Spa

Treatments at this spa are not focused on achieving outer beauty. Rather, the tailor-made spa experiences are meant to enhance health and wellness. It uses environmentally friendly products and each experience lasts long after guests leave. Try the Ayurvedic treatments. ◈ *J. W. Marriott Las Vegas, 221 N. Rampart Blvd • Map A3 • 702 869 7807*

Kim Vō Salon, Spa at The Mirage

3 The Spa at The Mirage

Feel your stresses and strains ebb away at this beautifully redesigned spa with its calming, neutral decor. There are additional treatment rooms and a more indulgent menu. Celebrity colorist, Kim Vō, has opened a salon just next door, including a barber shop for men. ◈ *The Mirage, 3400 Las Vegas Blvd S. • Map P1–2 • 702 791 7472*

4 Qua Baths & Spa at Caesars Palace

With a style that recaptures the glorious splendor that was ancient Rome, the spa incorporates Roman baths and other touches of imperial luxury. In addition to the myriad treatments on offer for both men and women, there are weight-training facilities, and several wet rooms. ◈ *3570 Las Vegas Blvd S. • Map P1–2 • 866 782 0655*

5 Drift Spa

Dark stones and sleek furnishings set the scene for a chic relaxation experience at Drift Spa. A rejuvenating menu is based on the traditions of Turkey, Tunisia, Morocco, and Spain. Couples especially will delight to find treatment rooms featuring private gardens. Other enticing features include hot and cool soaking pools, a traditional co-ed Turkish Hammam, and private outdoor garden lounges. ◈ *Palms Place, 4321 Flamingo Rd W. • Map B4 • 702 944 3219*

For more on hotel facilities See pp14–15, 20–23 & 32–33

Spa at Monte Carlo

Topline furnishings from across the globe and personalized service are hallmarks of this spa, which has a cozy and intimate atmosphere. Helio-therapy, body wraps, body scrubs, facials, and a variety of

Spa Bellagio

massages are on the menu of services. Use of the whirlpools, sauna and steam room is available for a small fee. ⑥ *Monte Carlo, 3770 Las Vegas Blvd S. • Map Q1–2 • 702 730 5590*

MGM Grand Spa

Pamper yourself with a "Dreaming Ritual" package, which offers a foot soak, massage, and mud therapy treatment set to Aboriginal music. Alternatively, the excel-lent body exfoliation services take place in a wet room and include use of a Vichy shower, while the Arabica coffee scrub is one of the signature services. You can purchase day passes for the workout room, sauna, and Jacuzzi. There's also a top hair salon overlooking the pool.
⑥ *MGM Grand, 3799 Las Vegas Blvd S. • Map R2 • 702 891 3077*

Spa Bellagio

This Italianate pampering palace combines the elegance of marble with cutting-edge fitness equipment. The spa's signature treatment is the Bellagio Stone Massage, which combines specially "harvested" stones prepared in a hydrobath with an energy-balancing technique to provide a thoroughly relaxing experience. Service is attentive.
⑥ *Bellagio, 3600 Las Vegas Blvd S. • Map Q1–2 • 702 693 7472*

The Spa at New York-New York

It will take far longer than a New York minute to enjoy all that is on offer at this revamped spa. Relaxing treatments include the Long Island Getaway Scrub, New York Minute Manicure, and the Traffic Stopper Facial. ⑥ *New York-New York, 3790 Las Vegas Blvd S. • Map R1–2 • 702 740 6955*

The Spa at Encore

For a truly lavish spa experi-ence, few places compare to the designer treatment rooms, garden villas, and couples' rooms here. No detail is overlooked.
⑥ *Encore Las Vegas, 3121 Las Vegas Blvd S. • Map N2 • 702 770 7070*

Left **Old West theme park, Bonnie Springs** Right **Rainbow Theatre**

Children's Attractions

Adventuredome

This indoor amusement park has an extensive array of rides and games designed to keep kids entertained for hours. They can ride the Canyon Blaster, a looping roller coaster, or get wet on a water flume ride, Rim Runner. ◈ *Circus Circus, 2800 Las Vegas Blvd S. • Map M–N2 • 702 794 3939 • Open daily, hours vary • Admission charge*

Siegfried & Roy's Secret Garden and Dolphin Habitat

These two attractions come as a package, combining education and entertainment. Watch the dolphins *(right)* from above then use the tunnel for underwater viewing. The Secret Garden is an oasis of trees and greenery, with unusual residents, including white tigers, panthers, leopards, and rare white lions. You are allowed to stay as long as you like.

Dolphin Habitat, The Mirage

◈ *The Mirage, 3400 Las Vegas Blvd S. • Map P1–2 • 702 791 7111 • Open 11am–6:30pm Mon–Fri, 10am–6:30pm Sat & Sun • Admission charge*

Rainbow Theatre

Children will be entertained by dramatizations of folk tales, children's classic plays, musical comedies, and fantasies such as *Charlotte's Web* and *Sleeping Beauty.* Performances of several works are presented each year. ◈ *800 S. Brush St. • Map B3 • Programs vary • 702 229 6553 • Admission charge*

Children's Park

This kid-friendly area at Town Square Las Vegas features a treehouse in a live oak tree, a huge playground and fun water features. A hedge maze has interactive animal topiaries, including an elephant, monkey, dolphin, and flamingo. Plenty of shade sails and an easily accessible water fountain make it easy to stay cool in summer. ◈ *6605 Las Vegas Blvd • Map C5*

SoBe Ice Arena

This NHL-regulation sized rink offers both figure skating and ice hockey facilities, as well as skate rental and lessons. ◈ *Fiesta Rancho Casino Hotel, 2400 N. Rancho Drive • Map B2 • 702 631 7000 • Admission charge*

Las Vegas Mini Gran Prix

Adult Gran Prix Cars, sprint karts, go karts, kiddie karts, plus the Dragon Coaster, Super Slide, and lots of arcade games make this a favorite off-Strip destination for Las Vegas kids as well as visitors. ⓢ *1401 N. Rainbow Blvd • Map A2 • 702 259 7000 • Open 10am–9pm daily (to 11pm Sat)*

Shark Reef Aquarium

North America's only predator-based aquarium has more than 2,000 animals in 1.6 million gallons of water. More than 100 species of sharks, as well as giant rays, piranha, jellyfish, and sawfish surround visitors as they walk through an underwater glass tunnel. ⓢ *Mandalay Bay, 3950 Las Vegas Blvd S. • Map R1–2 • 702 632 7777 • Open 10am–8pm Sun–Thu, 10am–10pm Fri–Sat • Admission charge*

Bonnie Springs and Old Nevada

This Old West theme park, which is 10 minutes west of Las Vegas, may lack the slickness typical of others in Las Vegas, but its rough-and-ready charm usually wins the children over. Among the best features are pony rides, a petting zoo, and stores with merchandise from the days of yore. ⓢ *16395 Bonnie Springs Rd • 702 875 4191 • Hours vary according to season • Admission charge*

Red Rock Lanes

This 72-lane bowling center comes equipped with a great sound system, lighting effects, fog machines, image generators, and disco balls to turn an ordinary afternoon into a party. It is the

Bowling at Red Rock Lanes

most expensive venue of its kind to be built in the USA. ⓢ *Red Rock Resort, 11011 W. Charleston Avenue • Map A3 • 702 797 7777 • Open 8am–2pm Mon–Thu, from 8am Fri, 24 hours Sat, to 2am Sun • Admission charge*

Flamingo Wildlife Habitat

Step through the doors into the Flamingo Wildlife Habitat and you'll be transported to a place of lush foliage, exotic birds, and other animals. The creatures all live on islands and in streams surrounded by stunning landscape and waterfalls, and are cared for by a team of experts. Walk among flamingos, swans, ducks, turtles and koi in this quiet escape from the otherwise hectic Las Vegas Strip. There are presentations at the island daily at 8:30am and 11am. ⓢ *Flamingo Las Vegas, 3555 Las Vegas Blvd S. • Map P2 • Open 24 hrs • Free*

AROUND TOWN

AROUND THE REGION

LAS VEGAS TOP 10

Left **Circus Circus** Center **Tower, The Venetian** Right **Fountains, Bellagio**

The Strip

WALK ALONG THE LAS VEGAS STRIP *and you'll see that some of the best things in Las Vegas life are free – especially when it comes to sightseeing and entertainment. It costs nothing to walk through the hotel-casinos, and you can window-shop to your heart's content in* their shopping promenades. The hotel architecture makes for an attraction in its own right: where else would you find an Egyptian sphinx, the canals of Venice, and a medieval castle in the same block? In addition, some hotel-casinos have free entertainment going on outside their doors.

Circus Circus

The Sirens of TI

🔟 Strip Sights

1. The Sirens of TI
2. Circus Circus
3. Fountains of Bellagio
4. Flamingo Wildlife Habitat
5. Luxor
6. The Forum Shops at Caesars
7. The Auto Collections at Imperial Palace
8. Shark Reef Aquarium at Mandalay Bay
9. Paris Las Vegas
10. The Mirage Volcano

Gondoliers, The Venetian

The Sirens of TI

This free show, staged in a cove built at the entrance to TI, is a favorite with visitors to Las Vegas. The 23-minute crowd-pleaser showcases the beguiling and beautiful "Sirens of TI," who tempt and lure a band of swashbuckling pirates. From lively sword fights and acrobatic feats of derring-do to dazzling pyrotechnics and a rousing song-and-dance finale, this show is a hit, drawing huge crowds to their evening performances.

⊘ *TI, 3300 Las Vegas Blvd S.* • *Map P2* • *Performances spring & summer: 7pm, 8:30pm, 10pm & 11:30pm daily; winter & fall: 5:30pm, 7pm, 8:30pm, & 10pm daily* • *Free*

Circus Circus

Over the course of more than 40 years, Circus Circus has entertained hundreds of thousands of spectators with their impressive shows. Stars have included the Flying Farfans of Argentina, the miniature-bicycle rider Charles Charles of Paris, and Russian acrobat Valerie Akishin. With performances taking place every half hour, you can pop back for different shows and catch a wide variety of acts.

⊘ *2880 Las Vegas Blvd S.* • *Map M–N2* • *Performances every half hour, 11am–midnight* • *Free*

Fountains of Bellagio

More than 1,000 fountains perform a water ballet above Lake Bellagio, in defiance of the parched, baking desert that surrounds the city. Soaring as high as 240 ft (73 m) in the air, the cascading water is choreographed to classical music. Bellagio and the other properties in the MGM MIRAGE group use incandescent lighting rather than neon, which makes the Italian village surrounding the lake a lovely backdrop for the dancing waters. ⊘ *3600 Las Vegas Blvd S.* • *Map Q1–2* • *Performances every half hour, 3–7pm Mon–Fri, noon–7pm Sat–Sun. Every 15 mins 7pm–midnight daily* • *Free*

Flamingo Wildlife Habitat

The 15-acre (6-ha) habitat at Flamingo Las Vegas *(below)*, improbably located in the heart of the Las Vegas Strip, is home to 70 birds, including Chilean flamingos and black swans, more than 300 fish, and 30 turtles. It is a welcome oasis in the often overwhelming desert environment. ⊘ *Flamingo Las Vegas, 3555 Las Vegas Blvd S.* • *Map P2* • *Open 24 hrs* • *Free*

For more on shows **See pp38–9**

The Auto Collections at Imperial Palace

An Expanding City

In the past, Las Vegas saw very rapid expansion, with the constant construction of hotels, condominiums, and shopping facilities. In the mid-2000s, the city hit a sharp economic decline and many projects were put on hold or abandoned altogether. Today, Las Vegas is starting to grow again, but this time growth is both cautious and calculated.

5 Luxor

A strikingly modern twist on an ancient classic, Luxor's unique 30-floor, black-glass pyramid is one of the most recognizable landmarks in Vegas. A life-size replica of the Great Temple of Ramses II is prominently featured inside the awe-inspiring atrium, which at 29 million cubic ft (820,000 cubic m) is one of the largest in the world. A 10-story sphinx (larger than the Egyptian original) guards the premises. Luxor is also home to Cirque du Soleil production, CRISS ANGEL Believe, and BODIES... The Exhibition. ⊗ Luxor Hotel & Casino, 3900 Las Vegas Blvd • Map R1 • 702 262 4444

6 The Forum Shops at Caesars

Use the first freestanding escalator of its kind in the United States to reach desired shopping destinations, or ride it just for fun. In the Roman Great Hall,

check out the 50,000 gallon saltwater aquarium, home to hundreds of colorful tropical fish. Divers feed the fish twice a day so keep your eyes open, especially in the afternoon. Some of the shops provide entertainment, but often the most fun can be had taking a break on a bench to watch the shoppers from around the world. (See also pp26–7.)

7 The Auto Collections at Imperial Palace

Perhaps the most fascinating aspect of this collection is that all the vehicles (more than 250) are for sale. Elvis Presley's 1972 Lincoln Continental and a 1965 Rolls Royce Silver Cloud III that was once owned by Lucille Ball are just two of the vehicles that have passed through these doors. Look out for free tickets at tourist-information stations, on the website, and in entertainment magazines. ⊗ Imperial Palace, 3535 Las Vegas Blvd S. • Map P2 • 702 794 3174 • Open 10am–6pm daily • Admission charge

8 Shark Reef Aquarium at Mandalay Bay

It is truly awe-inspiring to wander within the special walkways of the 1.3 million-gallon (5.9 million-liter) aquarium and observe the thousands of wonderful sea creatures swimming together. Look out for the arowana dragon fish – and, of course, 11 different species of shark. ⊗ Mandalay Bay, 3950 Las Vegas Blvd S. • Map R1–2 • Open 10am–8pm Sun–Thu, 10am–10pm Fri & Sat • Admission charge

For more on the Strip See pp8–9

9 Paris Las Vegas

The Eiffel Tower and Arc de Triomphe are faithfully and impressively reproduced at Paris Las Vegas, albeit on a smaller scale than the originals. Buy fresh baguettes from a street vendor, and nibble to the strains of tunes by the great Maurice Chevalier, as interpreted by a wandering accordionist. The toy shop is worth a stop too. ⊗ *3655 Las Vegas Blvd S.* • *Map Q2*

10 The Mirage Volcano

With displays like this, it is hardly surprising that The Mirage, when it was built in 1989, is said to have triggered the 1990s hotel-building boom. The man-made, multimillion-dollar volcano *(below)* spews fire 100 ft (30 m) into the air on the hour, from dusk to 11pm every evening. Ingenious lighting and steam effects convey the drama of lava flows, while loudspeakers broadcast vivid sound effects featuring the work of Grateful Dead drummer Mickey Hart. ⊗ *The Mirage, 3400 Las Vegas Blvd S.* • *Map P1–2* • *Erupts 6pm–midnight* • *Free*

A Day on the Strip

Morning

🕐 Start with breakfast in the delightful Verandah at Four Seasons Hotel Las Vegas, which is within **Mandalay Bay**. While there, visit **Shark Reef Aquarium**. Also within the hotel is the **House of Blues**, worth checking out for the excellent collection of American folk art.

Head north up the Strip to the **Flamingo Wildlife Habitat** at Flamingo Las Vegas *(see p71)* followed by a walk to **The Auto Collections at Imperial Palace** (car buffs may have to be removed forcibly!).

For lunch, cross over to Harrah's for the **Flavors Buffet** *(see p49)*.

Afternoon

At The **Forum Shops** you are liable to shed the shoppers in your party.

Next stop is **Circus Circus** *(see p71)*. It's a hike, so you may opt to take the Deuce bus, which stops along the Strip. After your trip there, you deserve a sugar break. Head for the Krispy Kreme doughnut shop and enjoy one of its legendary doughnuts. Newly fortified, explore Circus Circus (laugh at your stomach outline in the funhouse mirrors) and then walk back down to **TI** and watch **The Sirens** show.

Cross the street to Casino Royale, get a window table, and watch **The Mirage Volcano** erupt while you dine. For a nightcap, walk down to the Eiffel Tower at **Paris Las Vegas**, for the best view of **Fountains of Bellagio** *(see p71)*.

Price Categories

For a standard, double room per night (with breakfast if included), taxes, and extra charges.

$	under $50
$$	$50–$100
$$$	$100–$150
$$$$	$150–$200
$$$$$	over $200

Above **Caesars Palace**

TOP 10 Hotels

1 The Big Theme Hotels
Among the city's most extravagant hotels are the Bellagio *(see pp14–15)*, The Venetian *(pp20–21)*, and Caesars Palace *(p32)*. Those that are extraordinary in their dedication to a theme, are Paris *(p33)*, New York–New York *(p32)*, TI *(p33)*, and Excalibur *(p33)*.

2 Tropicana Las Vegas
A $180 million transformation has given this property a new look. ⊘ *3801 Las Vegas Blvd S. • Map R2 • 800 462 8767 • www.tropLV. com • $$$*

3 Harrah's
Friendly hotel with comfortable rooms. It is also possible to play keno through the room's TV set. ⊘ *3475 Las Vegas Blvd S. • Map P2 • 702 369 5000 • www.harrahs.com • $$*

4 Circus Circus
A vast property with child-friendly attractions. It also has the only RV park on the Strip. ⊘ *2880 Las Vegas Blvd S. • Map M–N2 • 702 734 0410 • www.circuscircus.com • $$*

5 Bally's
This hotel has a relaxed atmosphere, an Olympic-size swimming pool, and large, luxurious rooms, many with good views of the Strip. ⊘ *3645 Las Vegas Blvd S. • Map Q2 • 800 634 3434 • www. ballyslasvegas.com • $$*

6 Cosmopolitan
Opened in 2010, this 2,995-room hotel is chic and sophisticated. The three-tiered chandelier is the centerpiece of the property. ⊘ *3708 Las Vegas Blvd S. • Map Q1–2 • 702 698 7000 • www. cosmopolitanlasvegas.com • $$$$$*

7 The Mirage
Conveniently located in the center of the Strip, The Mirage is famous for its tropical atrium, pretty pool with cascading water-fall, and Siegfried & Roy's white tigers. ⊘ *3400 Las Vegas Blvd S. • Map P1–2 • 702 791 7111 • www.mirage.com • $$$$*

8 Monte Carlo
An elegant European theme is reflected in the large rooms, each with a marble bathroom. ⊘ *3770 Las Vegas Blvd S. • Map Q1–2 • 702 730 7777 • www.montecarlo.com • $$*

9 MGM Grand
Despite being one of the largest hotels in the world, MGM Grand maintains a relaxed ambience. It boasts a luxurious spa *(see p65)*. ⊘ *3799 Las Vegas Blvd S. • Map R2 • 702 891 7777 • www.mgmgrand.com • $$$*

10 Luxor
Its 30-story pyramid and giant sphinx have been Vegas landmarks since 1993. ⊘ *3900 Las Vegas Blvd S. • Map R1 • 702 262 4444 • www.luxor.com • $$$*

For more theme hotels **See pp32–3**

Left **A Vegas games arcade** Center **Las Vegas Mini Gran Prix** Right **Coney Island Emporium**

10 Game Arcades

Fun Dungeon
Traditional carnival attractions take on a new excitement in a resort featuring medieval knights racing around on their steeds. ◈ *Excalibur, 3850 Las Vegas Blvd S.* • *Map R1–2*

Insert Coins
Kids don't have to have all the fun! This video lounge and game bar mixes classic arcade games – Space Invaders, Frogger, Pacman, Tetris – with grown-up cocktail service. ◈ *512 Fremont St* • *Map K4*

Arcade at the Bellagio
Located near the Bellagio Gallery of Fine Art, this arcade offers a variety of racing and fighting video games. ◈ *Bellagio, 3600 Las Vegas Blvd S.* • *Map Q1–2*

Pinball Hall of Fame
This museum and pinball arcade features hundreds of classic and new games. Older pinball machines cost 25 cents to play and newer ones cost 50 cents. ◈ *1610 Tropicana Ave E.* • *Map R5*

Las Vegas Mini Gran Prix
With adult Gran Prix cars, go-karts, and kids' karts, and a large prize center, this is a popular place to spend the afternoon. ◈ *1401 N. Rainbow Blvd.* • *Map A2*

Hi Scores Bar-Arcade
Play classic video games for free and enjoy one of the many craft beers at this lively gaming lounge. ◈ *65 S. Stephanie St, Henderson*

Midway at Circus Circus
Games galore, plus an array of fun mirrors, hotdog stands, popcorn machines, and other carnival delights. ◈ *Circus Circus, 2880 Las Vegas Blvd S.* • *Map M–N2*

Coney Island Emporium
Try out Big Apple-themed versions of traditional games such as coin pitches and shooting galleries, with New York-style food close at hand. ◈ *New York–New York, 3790 Las Vegas Blvd S.* • *Map R2*

Time-Out Arcade
In addition to a bowling center, there are more than 50 video arcade games at Time-Out Arcade. ◈ *South Point Hotel, Casino & Spa, 9777 Las Vegas Blvd S.*

In-Room Video Games
Most major Strip hotels will rent or loan video-game equipment to guests with children. Since by law no child under the age of 12 should be left unsupervised in a game arcade (and there is also a curfew for under-18s), many parents want to take advantage of this useful service.

For more on activities for children **See pp66–7**

Left *The Sirens of TI* Right **The Forum Shops, Caesars Palace**

TOP 10 Free Entertainment

The Sirens of TI
Top of the bill is the spectacular siren show staged in the evening at the hotel entrance *(see p71)*. ◈ TI, 3300 Las Vegas Blvd S. • Map P2

Caesars Palace Grounds
When Caesars Palace opened in 1966, no one had ever seen anything quite like it. The grounds, studded with Roman-style statuary, were – and still are – enchanting. ◈ Caesars Palace, 3570 Las Vegas Blvd S. • Map P1–2

Paris Las Vegas
It may not be *quite* the real thing, but well-observed touches lend the place a characteristic *joie de vivre (see p73)*. ◈ Paris Las Vegas, 3655 Las Vegas Blvd S. • Map Q2

The Venetian's Gondoliers and Minstrels
The gondoliers sing as they pole their boats, and when not on the water they roam the casino harmonizing Italian arias. ◈ The Venetian, 3355 Las Vegas Blvd S. • Map P2

Flamingo Wildlife Habitat
A 15-acre outdoor space which is home to many species of birds and fish *(see p71)*. ◈ Flamingo Las Vegas, 3555 Las Vegas Blvd S. • Map P2

The Mirage Volcano
This is Las Vegas at its lavish best: after dark, on the hour, the "volcano" at The Mirage blows its top *(see p73)*. ◈ The Mirage, 3400 Las Vegas Blvd S. • Map P1–2

Silverton Aquarium
More than 4,000 tropical fish and other marine creatures live in this vibrant, living sea inside a 117,000-gallon (440,000-liter) saltwater aquarium. ◈ Silverton Hotel and Casino, 3333 Blue Diamond Rd • Map B–C6

Fountains of Bellagio
The breathtaking choreography of the fountain displays at Bellagio offers some of the best free entertainment in Las Vegas *(see p71)*. ◈ Bellagio, 3600 Las Vegas Blvd S. • Map Q1–2

M&M's World
Extraordinary as it seems, an entire attraction – including a 3-D movie – has been built around these tiny, candy-coated chocolates. ◈ Showcase Mall, 3785 Las Vegas Blvd S. • Map Q–R2

The Sphinx at Luxor
It would be a shame (if somewhat difficult) to miss the 10-story sphinx (larger than the original) guarding Luxor *(see p72)*. The best view of this landmark is as you come in to land at McCarran International Airport. ◈ Luxor Hotel & Casino, 3900 Las Vegas Blvd S. • Map R1

For more low-cost entertainment **See p82**

Left **The Mirage Volcano** Center **Fountain show, Bellagio** Right **MGM Grand's fiber-optic sign**

🔟 Places to People-Watch

1 Bellagio Lobby

Settle down on a sofa to watch the gold dripping from the jet set. Soothe your envy with piano music from the caviar bar, Petrossian, and the marvelous artistry of the ceiling. 🅂 *Bellagio, 3600 Las Vegas Blvd S. • Map Q1–2*

2 Fountains at Miracle Mile Shops

When shopping gets tiring, sit yourself down near the fountain in the heart of the Miracle Mile Shops at Planet Hollywood, and watch the lighted water effects set to original music. 🅂 *Planet Hollywood, 3667 Las Vegas Blvd S. • Map Q2*

3 Around the Casino Tables

The stars play at upscale casinos such as MGM Grand, Bellagio, and Caesars Palace; stargazers should aim, apparently, for 11pm to 1am on weekends.

4 Mon Ami Gabi

Take a table at the sidewalk café, soak up the atmosphere, and enjoy the view of Bellagio's fountain show. 🅂 *Paris Las Vegas Hotel, 3655 Las Vegas Blvd S. • Map Q2*

5 Footbridges along the Strip

You can hop across Las Vegas Boulevard without playing traffic roulette, and enjoy marvelous vantage points of the thronging mêlée below.
🅂 *Map N–R2*

6 Bodies . . . The Exhibition

Explore the beauty of the human body. This exhibit at Luxor *(see p72)* is dedicated to illustrating the wonders of our own bodies. It will inspire a curiosity and awe. 🅂 *Luxor Hotel & Casino, 3900 Las Vegas Blvd S. • Map R1*

7 Film Locations

Do some detective work on where the stars are each day by calling 702 486 2727. This number will tell you the daily casting calls and where filming is taking place.

8 Fiber-Optic Signs

An increasing number of supersize signs like the one at MGM are appearing on the Strip. Expect to see vivid, lifelike clips of performers and upcoming attractions. 🅂 *MGM Grand, 3799 Las Vegas Blvd S. • Map R2*

9 Third Floor of The Cosmopolitan

Take a seat in one of the comfy chairs near the pool table and watch people as they come and go from the resort's restaurants.
🅂 *3708 Las Vegas Blvd S. • Map Q1–2*

10 The Forum Shops at Caesars

The cafés and benches within the shopping complex are good for relaxation and people-watching *(see pp26–7)*.
🅂 *Caesars, 3570 Las Vegas Blvd S. • Map P1–2*

Left **Fremont Street Experience lights** Right **A Vegas pawn shop**

Downtown

OWNTOWN LAS VEGAS *is not a place of mega-story financial temples. Instead, it is a conglomeration of government buildings, carnival attractions, not-so-very-glamorous casinos, shops dealing in souvenirs, and unclaimed pawn shop miscellany. The heart of the area has a neon-lit row of casinos and, since the mid-1990s, free entertainment in the form of the Fremont Street Experience. This nightlife zone is here to stay, but a large-scale revitalization effort has also turned Downtown Las Vegas into a growing draw for arts, culture and entrepreneurship.*

Left **Fremont Street Experience** Right **Old Las Vegas Mormon Fort Historic State Park**

Downtown Sights

1. Downtown's Neon Lights
2. Fremont Street Experience
3. Downtown Casinos
4. View from Stratosphere Tower
5. Old Las Vegas Mormon Fort Historic State Park
6. Pawn Shops
7. Street Festivals
8. Vegas Vic Sign
9. The Mob Museum
10. Plaza Hotel & Casino

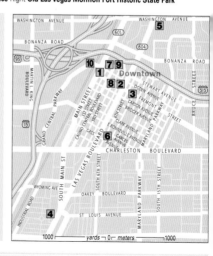

1 Downtown's Neon Lights

This area encompasses about eight blocks that front on Fremont Street, between Main and Fourth streets. Along this stretch is the most concentrated dazzle of neon on the planet. Not only are all the

Stratosphere Tower

Fremont Street casino fronts decorated with neon, but the street signs and light shows *(see p82)* above contribute to the sparkling brilliance. Night-time, of course, is when the lighting is at its most intense. The crowds on the malled walkway are heavy until after midnight, and the entertainment adds to a feeling of carnival. *(See also pp12–13)*.

2 Fremont Street Experience

The Fremont Street Experience encompasses an LED display canopy that is 1,500 ft (457 m) long, zip lines that are strung beneath the screen, and a pedestrian promenade. It comes alive at night with light and sound shows, and live entertainment *(see p82)*. Special events take place throughout the year, such as the St. Patrick's Day Celebration in March, Pride Parade in September, and a Veterans Day Parade in November. 🔊 *Fremont St between Main and 4th • Map K4*

3 Downtown Casinos

Along with all the outdoor activity on Fremont Street, there's action inside the casinos, too. They may not be as glamorous as the big hotels on the Strip, but the Fremont Street and other downtown

clubs have more history – some date back to the 1940s. They are also known for their bargain meals.

4 View from Stratosphere Tower

From the top of the tower on a clear day, parts of Arizona and California come into view. Count the 40 seconds it takes for the high-speed elevators to whiz up to the tower's floor-to-ceiling glass observation floor, which is 900 ft (275 m) above street level. The tower is a tourists' after-dark favorite for viewing the mesmerizing lights of downtown Las Vegas and the Strip. For a great view with an adrenaline rush, pay for one of the rides at the top. The Big Shot is a favorite. 🔊 *2000 Las Vegas Blvd S.* • *Map L–M3*

5 Old Las Vegas Mormon Fort Historic State Park

Mormons built the fort, along with a trading post in 1855, as a defense against the Native Americans (who turned out to be peaceful). It is the oldest building of its type in Nevada, but of the original structures, only a small adobe building that was part of the stockade remains.
🔊 *500 Washington Ave E.* • *Map J5*
• *Open 8am–5pm Mon–Fri* • *702 486 3511* • *Admission charge*

For more on Downtown Las Vegas **See pp12–13**

A night-time view of Downtown Las Vegas

Pawn Shops

Throughout downtown are several pawn shops, each with a unique selection of jewelry, electronics, trinkets, and other items. The most famous of these is Gold & Silver Pawn, which featured on the popular reality show Pawn Stars. There are often lines down the block of people waiting to get in. Stop by the Las Vegas Toy Shack on Fremont Street to meet the "toy guy" from Pawn Stars and check out vintage toys from yesteryear. ✆ 713 Las Vegas Blvd S. • Map K4

Street Festivals

Downtown Las Vegas' growth and revitalization has resulted in a number of street festivals. In the Arts District, First Friday invites people to explore the galleries and meet the artists. Vegas Streats is a gathering of the city's food trucks combined with live music and entertainment every second Saturday near El Cortez. ✆ First Fri, throughout downtown • Vegas Streats, 600 Fremont St at El Cortez • Map K4

New Year's Eve in Downtown Las Vegas

Historically, downtown has been the place favored by Las Vegas resident revelers for New Year's Eve. Each year since the advent of the Fremont Street Experience, the celebrations have become more elaborate with live music and other entertainment; food and beverages; a countdown to midnight; fireworks; and dancing in the streets. Of course, there are paper hats and noisemakers, too. But, unlike most Fremont Street happenings on all other days of the year, some of the New Year's Eve festivities are not free.

Vegas Vic Sign

Fifty feet (16 m) tall, Vegas Vic is a survivor from the early casino days. In bygone days not only did he smoke and wave but he also talked, saying "Howdy pardner, welcome to Las Vegas." Vic has now become an iconic Las Vegas symbol and the backdrop for thousands of visitors' photographs each year. ✆ 25 Fremont Street • Map K4

Mormon Fort

9 The Mob Museum

Las Vegas' notorious history is tied up in the Mob and on display at the old courthouse, one of the most historic buildings in Las Vegas. In addition to exhibits specific to Las Vegas, the museum examines organized crime on a larger scale, with artifacts and true-life accounts. A number of weapons, wiretapping tools and crime scene photos are displayed side by side with insider accounts into some of the biggest names of organized crime. These include Al Capone, Ben Siegel, Frank Rosenthal, and Whitey Bulger. The exhibit also examines popular myths about The Mob, separating fact from fiction, and what happens when notable figures retire, die, or go into the witness protection program. ◈ *300 Stewart Ave • Map J4*

10 Plaza Hotel & Casino

From Main Street, the Plaza may look like just another casino, but it sits on a historic spot. Built in the 1970s, the Plaza is located on the site of the birthplace of Las Vegas, at the first Union Pacific Railroad Depot Station. The station is no longer there, but the railroad tracks can still be seen on the back side of the property. The Plaza has the only bingo room in downtown Las Vegas. Bingo sessions are every two hours, beginning at 11am and ending at 9pm. ◈ *1 Main St at Fremont Street • Map J4*

Downtown After Dark

Late Afternoon

Begin your excursion in the mid- to late afternoon, with a visit to the **Mormon Fort** *(see p79)*. Allow more time if you are a history buff.

Next, explore Las Vegas' history with a visit to the **Neon Museum** *(see p45)* and **The Mob Museum**, both of which offer a peek into the past. Make plans in advance to ensure both are open.

For a special treat, try dining at one of the top restaurants in downtown, such as Vic & Anthony's at the Golden Nugget Casino (129 Fremont St), with its classy decor, or the romantic Hugo's Cellar at Four Queens (202 Fremont St).

Night-time

After dinner, stroll along Fremont Street's pedestrian promenade, stopping to watch people on the zip lines overhead and the buskers performing on the street. If gaming's your pleasure, step inside the El Cortez Hotel's casino (600 Fremont Street).

Check out the casino at the **Plaza**, then wander down to Main Street Station. Pick up a brochure here with a map and list of treasures – including street lamps from Brussels and a portion of the Berlin wall – that are incorporated into the building's decor.

Back at **Fremont Street Experience** *(p79)*, watch a light and sound show, then head to **Stratosphere** *(p79)* to top off the night with a stunning view of the city.

Left **Fremont Street Experience** Right **Musical street performers**

TOP 10 Low-Cost Food & Entertainment

1 Fremont Street Experience
Beginning at dusk, the Fremont Street light and sound shows bring the overhead canopy to life. The larger-than-life shows are four blocks long, and played out on 1.5 million LED lights. ⊗ Map K4

2 In-N-Out Burger
The nation's oldest drive-through burger chain is just the place for people who are hungry but don't have time to stop. Items on the restaurant's "secret," unpublished menu include a burger served "animal style" with a mustard-cooked beef patty and grilled onions. "Protein style" burgers come without a bun.
⊗ Multiple locations in Las Vegas

3 Golden Gate Shrimp Cocktails
For years, fresh shrimp cocktails have been the loss leader at the Golden Gate – they have sold more than 40 million. The cost: $2.99. ⊗ 1 Fremont Street • Map K4

4 People Watching
Because of its relaxed atmosphere, there are all sorts of interesting people downtown. Look up to watch the zip liners whiz by.

5 Sam Boyd's Margaritas
Connoisseurs swear that the 99-cent margaritas, served at all the casinos' bars, are as good as any you can find elsewhere at many times the price. ⊗ Sam Boyd's Fremont Hotel & Casino, 200 Fremont Street • Map K4

6 Aloha Specialties
A number of dishes are easy on the wallet, especially between the hours of 9am and 9pm. ⊗ California Hotel & Casino, 12 Ogden Ave E. • Map J4

7 Sourdough Cafe
A relic of a bygone era, this East Las Vegas casino's no-frills café serves eggs with ham or steak for $4.44 ($3.99 with player's card). ⊗ Arizona Charlie's Boulder Casino, 4575 Boulder Hwy • Map E4

8 Street Performers
Fremont Street is packed with musicians, artists, and people dressed in costume. Enjoy for free but leave a tip for photographs.

9 Penny Video Poker Machines
The penny slot machines of the early casinos have disappeared from all but a few places such as the Four Queens – you're more likely to spend 45 or even 90 cents with every pull. ⊗ Four Queens Hotel and Casino, 202 Fremont St • Map K4

10 Free Slot Pulls
It's easy to happen upon hotels along Fremont Street that offer free pulls on the slot machines. The goal is to get guests inside, but there is no obligation to stay.

Left **Vendor cart** Center **Bonanza Gift Shop** Right **The Funk House**

🔟 Places to Shop

1 Resnick's Grocery
Billed as an urban grocery with attitude, this store sells eco-friendly and organic products. Ⓢ *900 Las Vegas Blvd S. • Map J5*

2 The Funk House
Numerous 50s, 60s, and 70s goods, such as lamps, ceramics, paintings, rugs, advertising, jewelry, and toys. Novelties include a 1950s Coca-Cola vending machine and a vintage pedal car. The store is jam-packed, so take time to find the perfect treasure. Ⓢ *1228 S. Casino Center Blvd • Map L3*

3 The Attic
This claims to be the largest vintage clothing store in the world, where the young and hip make everything new again. Even the building has a distinctly retro feel. *(See also p91.)* Ⓢ *1010 N. Main Street • Map K3*

4 Gambler's General Store
An intriguing place even for non-gamblers, this huge store is devoted to gaming paraphernalia. There are dice tables, roulette wheels, antique slot machines, and the "shoes" from which cards are dealt in blackjack. Ⓢ *800 S. Main Street • Map K3*

5 Bonanza Gift Shop
The list of merchandise at this enormous store is as long as the souvenir manufacturers' imaginations. Anything at all that can be marketed as a memento of a visit to Las Vegas will be found here.

6 Las Vegas Premium Outlets
Close to downtown, this outlet park has more than 100 stores selling a range of clothing, household goods, gifts, jewelry, and food. High-end stores include Banana Republic, Coach, 7 For All Mankind, Burberry, and Armani Exchange. Ⓢ *875 S. Grand Central Parkway • Map K3*

7 Charleston Antique Mall
Located close to the Las Vegas Strip, this co-operative offers an endless assortment of antiques and vintage collectibles at incredible prices. Dealers bring merchandise in from far and wide. Ⓢ *560 S. Decatur Blvd • Map B3*

8 Beef Jerky Store
Smoked salmon, roasted soybeans, dried plums, glazed apricots, and *biscotti* are sold alongside dozens of varieties of jerky (sun-dried meat). Ⓢ *112 N. 3rd Street • Map K4*

9 Rainbow Feathers
Explore feather boas and an array of other colorful items at this store. Ⓢ *1036 S. Main Street • Map K3*

10 Vendors' Carts
Carts placed at intervals down the center of the Fremont Street mall offer sunglasses, wind chimes, stuffed toys, baseball caps, and mini-cars in various makes and models. Ⓢ *Map K4*

Left **Las Vegas Speedway** Center **Chinatown Plaza** Right **Henderson Farmers Market**

Beyond the Neon

LOOK BEYOND THE NEON and you will find that Las Vegas is, like the god Janus, a two-faced town. One is about make-up and make-believe; the other is like that of other American towns, with popular city parks, a thriving university, community centers, and playgrounds. Las Vegas is a city where significant research is undertaken at medical centers, and where cultural performances take place almost every night. It is also a growing city with many ethnic neighborhoods.

Left **Botanical gardens, UNLV** Right **UNLV campus**

🔟 Sights Beyond the Neon

1. Chinatown Plaza
2. Broadacres Marketplace & Event Center
3. UNLV Campus
4. Dig This
5. Ethel M Chocolate Factory
6. Las Vegas Motor Speedway
7. Masquerade Village
8. Sunset Park
9. Marjorie Barrick Museum of Natural History
10. Country Fresh Farmers Market

1 Chinatown Plaza

With pagoda-style roofs, a traditional Chinese entrance gate, and a statue of the mythical monk Tripitaka, with his companions – a pig, a soldier, and a monkey – Chinatown Plaza offers a delightful blend of East and West. Stores specialize in both American and Eastern necessities and Asian luxuries. Chinese music wafts through the covered walkways, and art throughout the Plaza spotlights Chinese customs and traditions. Not surprisingly, this is the place to come for the best Asian cuisine in town. There are Filipino, Korean, Japanese, and Vietnamese restaurants, in addition to Chinese establishments. ◎ *4255 Spring Mountain Rd • Map B–C4*

2 Broadacres Marketplace & Event Center

This swap meet brings together more than 1,150 vendors selling antiques, toys, crafts, shoes, and electronics. Although most items are priced, feel free to bargain for a better deal. On weekends, live bands play on a large stage with a covered seating area. The food options are plentiful, with stalls selling everything from burritos to barbecue fare. ◎ *2390 Las Vegas Blvd N. • Map D2*

3 UNLV Campus

City residents' favorite areas for taking a walk include the campus of the University of Nevada Las Vegas, which was established in 1957. The university may not have any remarkable buildings, but there are shade trees, and in early evening the paths are blissfully uncrowded. Be sure not to miss the desert garden, which is lovely. Summer days are much warmer than winter days, but the campus is less crowded in the summer. ◎ *S. Maryland Parkway • Map Q4*

4 Dig This

For those who have always wanted to experience working at a construction site, this heavy equipment playground is a dream. Choose a bulldozer or excavator, go through an orientation exercise, then participate in one of the many activities such as building mounds, stacking tires, and digging deep trenches. If time permits, visitors receive free time in their machines to play as they choose. Book in advance to ensure your equipment is available. Participants must be aged 14 or above and be at least 48 in (122 cm) tall. ◎ *3012 Rancho Dr • Map N1*

Chinatown Plaza

Casinos Beyond the Neon

Although for the past few decades Las Vegas has been a sprawling city with shopping centers and clusters of businesses in the various neighborhoods, almost all of the hotel/casinos were concentrated in two areas – downtown and along the Strip. In the 1980s, when the city's population began its explosive growth, a number of neighborhood hotel/casinos were built. Visitors who venture beyond the neon for gaming may be pleasantly surprised to find a friendly atmosphere and lovely surroundings (see p88).

Las Vegas Motor Speedway

Ethel M Chocolate Factory

Take a free tour to view the glass-enclosed, spotless, white kitchens where the diligent candy-makers concoct their sweet creations. Find out what the large stainless steel machines do, and admire the finished confections wrapped in their foil of emerald, ruby, sapphire, and other jewel colors. Every tour participant receives a free chocolate at the end of the tour. Outside the factory is a lovely cactus garden, with plants clearly identified.
◎ 2 Cactus Garden Drive, Henderson • Map E5 • Open 8:30am–6pm daily • Free

Las Vegas Motor Speedway

Completed in 1996, the 142,000-seat Las Vegas Motor Speedway was the first new super-speedway to be built in the southwest USA in more than two decades. The 1,600-acre facility has 14 different race tracks, food courts, three levels of open-air grandstand viewing, VIP party rooms, and 102 luxury skybox suites. Important races staged here include NASCAR and NHRA events. Visitors can take a lesson in racecar driving at the Richard Petty Driving Experience. Concerts are sometimes held here as well.
◎ 7000 Las Vegas Blvd N. • 702 644 4444 • Map E1 • Call for opening times

Masquerade Village

The complex is designed to resemble an idyllic fishing village in northern Italy. Shop, drink and dance the night away at this all-in-one party destination, located in the eye-catching hotel, the Rio. Weekends are especially great, with free concerts and party bands that play some of today's greatest hits. ◎ Rio All-Suite Hotel & Casino, 3700 W. Flamingo Rd • Map P1 • 888 396 2483 • Free shows 9pm–12am Fri & Sat

Ethel M Chocolate Factory

Sunset Park
One of the city's most popular parks, Sunset offers basketball, tennis, and jogging *(see p61)*; a place to fly kites and sail boats and some of the best picnic spots in town. It also has a well-kept dog park, popular with local dog walkers. ◈ *2601 E. Sunset Rd* • *Map D5*

Marjorie Barrick Museum
The museum centers around desert animals and insects native to the southwest, as well as art. It also contains exhibits on the area's anthropology, archeology, and early-day architecture. ◈ *UNLV campus* • *Map Q4* • *702 895 3381* • *Open 10am–6pm Tue, Wed, Fri; 10am–8pm Thu; 10am–4pm Sat & Sun* • *Free (contributions suggested)*

Country Fresh Farmers Market
Henderson's market had its beginnings in 1999 and gets bigger each season. Farmers drive from the California valleys to sell their produce year-round; in the summer season, they're joined by Nevada growers. Artisans sell everything from hand-painted china and rag dolls to house plants and chess sets. ◈ *240 Water St (Thu), 200 S. Green Valley Pkwy (Fri)* • *702 579 9661* • *Open 9am–4pm Thu, 10am–4pm Fri*

Sunset Park

Two Excursions Beyond the Neon

Morning
Begin with an early morning stroll around the UNLV campus, stopping at the **Marjorie Barrick Museum.**

Drive to **Town Square Las Vegas** *(see p66)* where, if children are in your party, the play equipment will be the main attraction. Don't miss the shops while you're there! Then it's on to the **Ethel M Chocolate Factory** for the free tour and walk around the cactus garden. Buy some chocolate for a local souvenir.

Before lunch, head to **Broadacres Marketplace** for eclectic shopping and people watching, then stop by Chinatown Plaza for a bite to eat with Asian flair *(see p85).*

Afternoon
Begin at the **Nevada State Museum and Historical Society** *(see p85)* to learn more about the Silver State. Motor-racing fans should then make their next stop the **Las Vegas Motor Speedway**.

Those who want to try their hand at driving heavy equipment should stop by **Dig This** for an exhilarating experience. If you still have any energy left, **Sunset Park** is a great place to take a run or some time to relax if you prefer. Other outdoor areas offer opportunities for disc golf, hiking, and cycling *(see pp60–1)*. In the evening, visit a "local's casino" away from the Strip for a different dining and gaming experience.

Left **JW Marriott Las Vegas, housing Rampart Casino** Center **Sunset Station** Right **Texas Station**

TOP 10 Casinos

1 Rio All-Suite Hotel & Casino
The Rio has more video poker machines than most, and a friendly feeling associated with casinos that rely on local trade for repeat business. *(See also p36.)* ✆ 3700 W. Flamingo Rd • Map P1 • 888 396 2483

2 Rampart Casino
An intimate gaming atmosphere with a relaxing, upscale casino floor away from the crowds of the Strip. *(See also p36.)* ✆ 221 N. Rampart Blvd • Map A3 • 702 869 7777

3 Santa Fe Station
A mid-size gambling floor (2,900 slots), the Santa Fe is patronized primarily by locals and is one of the more pleasant casinos beyond the neon. *(See also p36.)* ✆ 4949 N. Rancho Drive • Map A1 • 800 678 2846

4 Green Valley Ranch Resort
Inspired by the great casinos of Europe, Green Valley has over 2,000 games machines and 55 table games. ✆ 2300 Paseo Verde Parkway, Henderson • 702 617 7777

5 Fiesta Rancho
From cocktail waitresses in jewel-toned satin outfits to the gaily patterned carpets on the floor, the casino evokes party time. *(See also p37.)* ✆ 2400 N. Rancho Drive • Map B2 • 702 631 7000

6 Texas Station
The theme is of a 19th-century town in the Lone Star state of Texas, with wagon wheels and gunpowder barrels. ✆ 2101 N. Rancho Drive • Map B2 • 702 631 1000

7 Sunset Station
Mediterranean-themed casino with wrought-iron balconies. Natural light makes it more pleasant than most. ✆ 1301 W. Sunset Rd, Henderson • Map F6 • 702 547 7777

8 Sam's Town
One of the largest non-Strip casinos with thousands of slots, video poker, and keno machines. ✆ 5111 Boulder Hwy, Las Vegas • Map E4 • 702 456 7777

9 The Orleans
There's a feeling of Mardi Gras in the casino, which is patterned after New Orleans' Vieux Carré. ✆ 4500 W. Tropicana Ave • Map B4 • 702 365 7111

10 Arizona Charlie's
Dude-ranch touches include deer antler chandeliers. Pai gow poker and Royal Match 21 are included in the games. ✆ 740 S. Decatur Blvd • Map B3 • 702 258 5200

For more hotels and casinos in Las Vegas **See pp32–7**

Left **Polo Towers** Right **Rio All-Suite Hotel & Casino**

Hotels and Motels

1 JW Marriott Las Vegas
This resort has lush grounds filled with pools and trees. Guests enjoy top golf courses, a relaxing spa, and great restaurants including Gustav Mauler's Spiedini. *221 N. Rampart Blvd • Map A3 • 702 869 7777 • $$$$*

2 Rumor
Awash in modern style, Rumor is one of the few boutique hotels in Las Vegas. It is also pet-friendly. *455 E. Harmon Ave • Map Q3 • 702 369 5400 • $$*

3 Polo Towers
Resort condominiums offering nightly rentals when the accommodations are not occupied by vacation ownership members. Great for families. *3745 Las Vegas Blvd S. • Map Q2 • 800 935 2233 • $$$*

4 Rio All-Suite Hotel & Casino
Perfect for visitors who want the total resort experience without the congestion of the Strip. *(See also p33.)* *3700 Flamingo Rd W. • Map P1 • 888 396 2483 • $$$*

5 Palms Casino Resort
Palms' offers stunning views of Las Vegas. Its Hardwood Suite is a big draw. *4321 W. Flamingo Rd • Map B4 • 702 942 7777 • $$$*

6 Artisan
A non-gaming property, Artisan has a stylish nightclub and restaurant. *1501 Sahara Ave W. • Map M2 • 702 214 4000 • $$$$$*

7 The Orleans
French Quarter-themed hotel, with green-shuttered windows and wrought-iron balconies. *4500 W. Tropicana Ave • Map B4 • 702 365 7111 • $$*

8 Sunset Station
Experience almost all the Las Vegas diversions in an away-from-the-Strip location: shopping at the Galleria *(see p52)*, golf, and casino action. *1301 W. Sunset Rd, Henderson • Map F6 • 702 547 7777 • $$*

9 M Resort
This 390-room upscale resort is located 10 miles (16 km) south of the Strip. It offers stunning, uninterrupted views of the Las Vegas Valley, as well as several dining options and a world-class spa *(see p37)*.

10 Santa Fe Station
A hit with people who love active vacations, with a 60-lane bowling alley and line-dancing lessons. Golf packages are also available. *4949 N. Rancho Drive • Map A1 • 800 678 2846 • $$*

Price Categories

For a three course	
meal for one with a	**$** under $20
half bottle of wine (or	**$$** $20–$30
equivalent meal), taxes	**$$$** $30–$45
and extra charges.	**$$$$** $45–$60
	$$$$$ over $60

Left **Wienerschnitzel** Right **Hard Rock Café**

Around Town – Beyond the Neon

Family Restaurants

Fatburger
Big, handmade burgers, hearty fries, and a classic 1950s atmosphere make Fatburger a top Las Vegas hamburger destination. A rock 'n' roll jukebox adds a note of authenticity and old-fashioned charm to the decor. ✆ *3763 Las Vegas Blvd S. (and other locations)* • Map R2 • 702 736 4733 • $

Hard Rock Café
Huge three-decker bacon, lettuce, and tomato sandwiches, great hamburgers, and fresh apple cobbler. ✆ *3771 Las Vegas Blvd S.* • Map Q2 • 702 733 7625 • $$$

Original Pancake House
The portions are huge; the pancakes, divine. And so many varieties – blueberry, apple, plate-size German pancakes, or buttermilk hotcakes as small as silver dollars. ✆ *4170 S. Fort Apache Rd* • 702 433 5800 • $

Omelet House
This low-key breakfast spot serves the under-10 crowd meals big enough to satisfy an adult. ✆ *2160 W. Charleston Blvd* • Map L2 • 702 384 6868 • $

Wienerschnitzel
Drive-thru hotdog stand, with both the traditional pickles-with-mustard dogs and variations. ✆ *4680 E. Flamingo Rd (and other locations)* • Map E4 • 702 362 0418 • $

Romano's Macaroni Grill
Bruschetta with a selection of toppings, fried mozzarella cheese, Italian *panini* sandwiches, and mouth-watering pasta. ✆ *2400 W. Sahara* • Map C3 • 702 248 9500 • $$

Lotus of Siam
One of the finest Thai restaurants in Vegas, known for its excellent service. ✆ *953 E. Sahara Ave* • Map M4 • 702 735 3033 • $$$

BJ's Restaurant & Brewhouse
Salads, sandwiches, pastas, and steaks, but the main draw are the gourmet pizzas. The lunch specials are excellent. ✆ *10840 W. Charleston Ave* • 702 853 2300 • $$

Mimi's Café
Comfort food served in a warm atmosphere. Meals are large and filling. ✆ *6790 N. Durango Dr* • 702 645 3688 • $$

Buca di Beppo
There are family-style platters and hefty bottles of wine to be had at this authentic Italian dining experience. ✆ *412 East Flamingo Rd* • Map Q3 • 702 866 2867 • $$$

For salad bars, buffets, and brunches See pp48–9

Left **Indoor Swap Meet** Right **Chinatown Plaza**

TOP 10 Shopping

1 Chinatown Plaza
A shopping center that serves the needs of the city's sizeable Asian community as well as Asian-American tourists and visitors from around the world. At festival times *(see p58)*, counters are piled high with moon cakes and treats linked to special days. *(See also p85.)*

2 The Attic
The largest vintage clothing store in the world, with 1940s pillbox hats and rhinestone jewelry, 1960s tuxedos, and 1950s-style hot pants and sequined eyeglasses. Ⓢ *1010 N. Main St • Map K3 • www.atticvintage.com*

3 Antique Mall of America
More than 100 booths with an eclectic mix of antiques, collectibles, jewelry, furniture, and more. Ⓢ *9151 Las Vegas Blvd S.*

4 Las Vegas Premium Outlets
A truly fabulous place for any shoppers in your party who may have "champagne" tastes but "house-wine" wallets. Ⓢ *7400 Las Vegas Blvd S. • Map C6*

5 Fantastic Indoor Swap Meet
The swap meet is the American equivalent of the European flea market: vintage kitchen appliances, tire chains, home-baked bread, mismatched chairs, etc. Ⓢ *1717 S. Decatur Blvd • Map B3 • Open Fri–Sun*

6 Cost Plus World Market
Import bazaar with handsome tableware, furniture, foodstuffs, and art objects from all corners of the world. Ⓢ *2151 N. Rainbow Blvd • Map A2*

7 Sheplers
Nevada cowboys buy their bolo ties, boots, sheepskin jackets, big belt buckles, and cowboy hats here. Ⓢ *4700 W. Sahara Ave • Map B3*

8 Total Wine
A massive store featuring 8,000 wines, 3,000 spirits, and 2,500 beers. The staff are very knowledgeable. Ⓢ *730 Rampart Blvd*

9 Bell, Book, & Candle
Talismans, crystal balls, tarot cards, and other soothsayers' tools. Witchcraft lessons, too. Ⓢ *1725 E. Charleston Blvd • Map D3*

10 Susie's Deals
A big variety of clothing that caters for the whole family. The prices are reasonable, too. Ⓢ *1159 E. Twain Ave • Map P4*

For more on shopping **See pp52–5, 83 & 116**

Left **Hoover Dam** Center **Boulder City/Hoover Dam Museum** Right **Lake cruiser, Lake Mead**

Lake Mead, Hoover Dam, and Laughlin

T HE HOOVER DAM, MOST ASSUREDLY, *changed the face of the American West. Not only did it enable the production of vast amounts of electrical energy and help control floods, but it also provides water to cities and farms throughout the American Southwest and Mexico. The project's commercial byproducts in Nevada – Lake Mead and Boulder City, and the resort city of Laughlin – have infused billions of dollars into the state's economy and provided recreational opportunities for hundreds of millions of visitors.*

Left **View from Hoover Dam Visitor Center** Right **Lake Mead**

Sights Around Lake Mead and Laughlin

1. Hoover Dam Tour
2. Boulder City Historic District
3. Boulder City/Hoover Dam Museum
4. Lake Mead National Recreation Area
5. Lake Mead Marinas and Beaches
6. Laughlin's Casino Row
7. Lake Mohave
8. Petroglyphs near Laughlin
9. Oatman, Arizona
10. Avi Resort and Casino

Hoover Dam Tour

Hoover Dam Tour
Begin a visit in the three-story visitor center perched on the Nevada canyon wall. From here, Bureau of Reclamation guides offer tour options into the hydro-powerplant or the dam itself. Enjoy audio and film presentations, exhibits, and other media that tell the story of the Colorado River's settlement and the facts behind the technology involved in the distribution of water and production of hydro-electric power. Catch the view from the top of the center to see the face of the dam, Lake Mead behind it, and the Colorado River below it. *(See also p10.)* ⊗ *Visitor Center, Hoover Dam • 702 494 2517 • Tour reservations 866 730 9097*

Boulder City Historic District
It's worth including Boulder City on a Hoover Dam trip to appreciate the scale of work involved – the city was built as a model community to house dam construction workers. The grandest buildings are the Bureau of Reclamation and the Bureau of Light headquarter buildings; the Municipal Building; and the Boulder Dam Hotel. Most of the construction, however, was focused on the two- and three-room houses for the workers. *(See also p11.)* ⊗ *Information from Hoover Dam Museum • Hwy 93 at Lakeshore Rd • 702 294 1988*

Boulder City/ Hoover Dam Museum
Built in 1933, the Dutch Colonial-style Boulder Dam Hotel now houses the Boulder City/Hoover Dam Museum. Actor Boris Karloff and other Hollywood stars stayed in the hotel's glory days, and Crown Prince Olav and Princess Martha of Norway hosted a party here in 1939. The out-of-town hotel declined in the postwar rise of Las Vegas as a tourist mecca, but, since the mid-1990s, a group of volunteers has set about rehabilitating it. The museum itself includes memorabilia from the 1930s. *(See also p11.)* ⊗ *1305 Arizona St, Boulder City • 702 294 1988 • Open 10am–5pm Mon–Sat • Admission charge*

Lake Mead National Recreation Area
After the completion of the Hoover Dam in 1935, the waters of the Colorado River filled the deep canyons that once towered above the river to create a huge reservoir. This lake, with its 550 miles (1,120 km) of shoreline, is the centerpiece of Lake Mead National Recreation Area, a 2,300-sq mile (6,000-sq km) tract of land. ⊗ *Information from Alan Bible Visitor Center • 601 Nevada Way, Boulder City • 702 293 8990 • www.nps.gov/lake*

Boulder City Historic District

For more on the Hoover Dam See pp10–11

Around the Region – Lake Mead, Hoover Dam, and Laughlin

Don Laughlin opened his four-unit motel and bar with about a dozen slot machines on the banks of the Colorado River in the same week in 1966 as the opulent Caesars Palace opened in Las Vegas. Laughlin town (named by the postmaster in 1977) is now Nevada's third busiest gambling destination – outranked only by Las Vegas and Reno.

Casino Row, Laughlin

may not be as dazzling as those along the Las Vegas Strip, but they offer extremely good value. Getting around is easier than in Las Vegas: a riverwalk connects most of the casinos, or you can take a bus or shuttle boat. Tours of the Colorado River are also available.
⊗ 90 miles (145 km) S. of Las Vegas
• www.visitlaughlin.com

Lake Mead Marinas and Beaches

Lake Mead's marinas and beaches range from delightful tiny coves to long stretches of sand. Popular areas include Lake Mead RV Village, Echo Bay, Boulder Beach, Lake Mead Marina, and Temple Bar. These have recreational vehicle sites with full hookups, and supplies at nearby stores. Boxcar and Icebox coves are favorites with houseboaters. Callville Bay, Las Vegas Boat Harbor, and Lake Mead marinas are close to Hoover Dam, while Temple Bar marina serves the lake's southeast reaches. ⊗ Information from Alan Bible Visitor Center • 702 293 8990

Laughlin's Casino Row

The establishments lining Laughlin's South Casino Drive

Lake Mohave

The 67-mile (107-km) long lake extends from below Hoover Dam to Davis Dam, 2 miles (3.5 km) north of Laughlin, and is only 4 miles (6.5 km) across at its widest point. A National Park Service Visitor Center at Katherine Landing, just north of Laughlin, offers free guided walks by park rangers. Boat rentals and fishing tackle are available at Katherine Landing, Willow Beach Marina, and Cottonwood Cove. Record-size striped bass have been caught in Lake Mohave. ⊗ Part of Lake Mead National Recreation Area • Admission fee to park • www.nps.gov/lake

Petroglyphs near Laughlin

Christmas Tree Pass and Grapevine Canyon, just west of Laughlin on Hwy 163, are the best places to see the fascinating petroglyphs incised into the cliffs of the canyons by the early Patayan group.

Echo Bay, Lake Mead

The line drawings and symbols may have served as the road maps of their day, directing hunters and fishermen. National Park Service personnel have located more than 150 Patayan camp sites between Davis Dam and Willow Beach, which is 10 miles (16 km) from the base of Hoover Dam. Ⓝ *Part of Lake Mead National Recreation Area* • www.nps.gov/lake

Petroglyph near Laughlin

9 Oatman, Arizona
A century ago, Oatman was a thriving gold mining center; today, visitors are taken back to the old days of the Wild West, with burros roaming the streets and staged gunfights in the middle of town. The Oatman Hotel was where honeymooners Clark Gable and Carole Lombard stayed in 1939. The town has been used as the location for a number of movies, including *How the West Was Won*.
Ⓝ *General information 928 768 6222*

10 Avi Resort and Casino
In 1995, the Fort Mojave Indian tribe opened Nevada's first Native American-owned casino and the only Native American-owned gaming business in the USA operated under state regulations. "Avi" means money or loose change. The resort is located in an area that the tribe intends to develop as a planned community. *(See also p97.)*

Two Days at the Dam and Laughlin

Day One

🕐 Begin with early morning coffee at Railroad Pass Casino on Hwy 93, an old-timer among gambling dens. Afterward, continue on Hwy 93 to the historic **Boulder City** and **Hoover Dam** *(see p93)* for the amazing tour.

Go back along Hwy 93 to the junction with Hwy 95 and turn south toward Laughlin. Stop at the **Nugget** in Searchlight *(see p96)* for lunch and the chance to visit a typical small-town Nevada casino.

For a more picturesque route, turn off 95 and head east on the dirt road through Christmas Tree Pass. Spend the remainder of the day in **Laughlin**, perhaps hunting for bargains at the 50-store Laughlin Outlet Center.

Overnight at **Harrah's** *(see p97)* or another hotel along the river, and be sure to take an evening stroll along the riverwalk.

Day Two

Early next morning, golfers can tee off at any of the six area championship golf courses, where you can golf in three states (Nevada, Arizona, and California).

Later, head for **Oatman**, an old-time western town about a half-hour's drive southeast from Bullhead City. In the afternoon drive back north to **Lake Mohave**. Be sure to make time to see the mysterious **petroglyphs** at Grapevine Canyon, off Hwy 163, before returning to your hotel in Laughlin.

Left **Nugget Restaurant, Searchlight** Right **Boulder Dam Brewing Company, Boulder City**

🔟 Places to Eat

1 Boulder Dam Brewing Company, Boulder City
A family-owned eatery serving fresh brews and great food. The walls are adorned with artifacts from the construction of the dam. There is also a lovely beer garden. ⓢ *453 Nevada Hwy • 702 243 2739 • $*

2 Toto's Mexican Restaurant, Boulder City
Mexican standards – burritos, tacos, enchiladas – done with flair at this popular chain. ⓢ *806 Buchanan Blvd • 702 293 1744 • $*

3 Nugget Restaurant, Searchlight
Dominated by a mural of the *Searchlight*, an 1880s riverboat. The signature dish is a jumbo corn muffin with sausage, scrambled eggs, and gravy. ⓢ *100 Highway 95 • 702 297 1201 • $*

4 The Steakhouse, Laughlin
Resembling a Victorian railroad parlor car, The Steakhouse has a romantic, intimate ambience and a contemporary dining menu. ⓢ *Tropicana Express Hotel & Casino, 2121 S. Casino Drive • 888 888 8695 • $$$*

5 The Lodge, Laughlin
Delicious American cuisine is served under open-beam ceilings and in front of a roaring fire. ⓢ *River Palms Resort Casino, 2700 S. Casino Drive • 800 835 7903 • $$*

6 Fresh Market Square Buffet, Harrah's, Laughlin
Offering 11 action cooking stations and themed areas including Mexican, sushi, Italian, seafood, and American. ⓢ *2900 S. Casino Drive • 702 298 4600 • $$*

7 Saltgrass Steak House
A popular local steakhouse that attracts a host of families regularly. Affordable prices and cowboy-themed dishes, such as the "Cowboy Ribeye". ⓢ *2300 S. Casino Drive • 702 298 7153 • $$$*

8 Milo's Cellar, Boulder City
This sidewalk café, wine bar, and liquor store serves a variety of gourmet sandwiches, antipasti, and cheese platters, as well as hundreds of wines and over 50 types of beer. ⓢ *538 Nevada Hwy • 702 293 9540 • $*

9 Joe's Crab Shack, Laughlin
This seafood restaurant has indoor seating with a casual atmosphere or outdoor seating under a covered patio. ⓢ *Golden Nugget, 2300 S. Casino Drive • 702 298 7143 • $$*

10 The Prime Rib Room, Laughlin
Prime rib carved tableside is the specialty here. Other entrées include chicken and fish. ⓢ *Riverside Casino, 1650 S. Casino Drive • 702 298 2535 • $*

The Steakhouse, Laughlin

Price Categories

For a standard, double room per night (with breakfast if included), taxes, and extra charges.

$	under $50
$$	$50–$100
$$$	$100–$150
$$$$	$150–$200
$$$$$	over $200

Left **Harrah's, Laughlin** Right **Golden Nugget, Laughlin**

TOP 10 Places to Stay and Casinos

1 Harrah's, Laughlin
Spanish-themed property with its own sand beach, a casino with windows looking out on the river, five restaurants, and a particularly pleasant ambience. ⊗ 2900 S. Casino Drive • 702 298 4600 • www.harrahslaughlin.com • $

2 Golden Nugget, Laughlin
A tropical atrium with cascading waterfalls, palm trees, and 300 species of tropical plants sets this hotel apart. The casino, with its 24 Karat Slot Club, is more attractive than most. ⊗ 2300 S. Casino Drive • 702 298 7111 • $$

3 Don Laughlin's Riverside Resort, Laughlin
A total destination resort. Unusual features include two classic auto showrooms and an antique slot machine display. There's also an RV park with full hook-ups. ⊗ 1650 S. Casino Drive • 702 298 2535 • $

4 Aquarius Casino Resort, Laughlin
The hotel features a large pool deck overlooking the river and Arizona hills, three lighted tennis courts, a wedding chapel, and Laughlin's largest tour boat, the *Celebration.* ⊗ 1900 S. Casino Drive • 702 298 5111 • $

5 Colorado Belle, Laughlin
Overlooking the Colorado River, this resort is housed in a replica paddlewheel boat and boasts the only microbrewery in Laughlin, Pints Brewery. Special events and performances occur frequently. ⊗ 2010 S. Casino Drive • 702 298 4000 • www.colorado-belle.com • $

6 Avi Resort and Casino, near Laughlin
Native American-owned resort *(see p95)* with a large, sandy, riverside beach, video arcade, swimming pool, live entertainment, and 29 spa suites. ⊗ 10 000 Aha Macav Parkway • 702 535 5555 • $

7 Quality Inn, Lake Mead
A 70-room motor hotel with views of Lake Mead. ⊗ 110 Ville Drive • 702 293 6444 • $$

8 El Rancho Boulder Motel, Boulder City
Spanish-style motel on the main street. Some rooms have kitchens. ⊗ 725 Nevada Hwy • 702 293 1085 • www.elranchoboulder.com • $$

9 Callville Bay, Lake Mead
The campground offers showers, restrooms, a restaurant, lounge, and fuel. Reservations are not accepted. ⊗ On the north side of Boulder Basin • 702 565 8958 • $

10 Seven Crown Resorts, Lake Mohave
Houseboats in various sizes and with excellent facilities can be rented here. All houseboaters have to bring on deck are food and clothing. ⊗ 2690 E. Katherine Spur Rd, Bullhead City • 800 752 9669 • $$$$$

Note: All hotels listed accept credit cards, have air-conditioning, and rooms with private bathrooms

Left **Petroglyphs, Valley of Fire** Center **Death Valley** Right **Scotty's Castle, Death Valley**

Parks and Preserves

L ESS THAN AN HOUR *from the man-made extravaganzas and simulations of the Strip are natural wonders so dramatic and thrilling that humans could not begin to replicate them. Many of these wonders are geological.* The closest is Red Rock Canyon (see pp24–5). Also nearby are Zion National Park, with its fantastic rock formations, and Death Valley – the hottest place in North America – whose floor lies 282 ft (85 m) below sea level, making it the lowest elevation in the western hemisphere. Most famous is undoubtedly Grand Canyon, whose dimensions are breathtaking. Each region has its distinct flora and fauna, with some species found nowhere else on Earth.

🔟 Sights of the Parks and Preserves

1 Petroglyph Canyon, Valley of Fire

2 Lost City Museum of Archeology, Overton

3 Kolob Canyons, Zion National Park

4 Zion Canyon

5 Bright Angel Point, North Rim, Grand Canyon

6 Yavapai Geology Museum, Grand Canyon

7 Watchtower, Grand Canyon

8 Scotty's Castle, Death Valley

9 Aguereberry Point, Death Valley

10 Dante's View, Death Valley

Zion Lodge, Zion Canyon

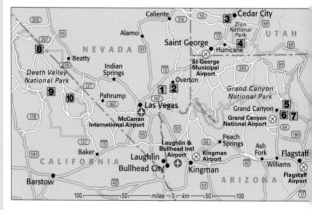

For more on the Grand Canyon See pp16–19

Left **Petroglyph Canyon** Right **Grand Canyon Lodge, North Rim, Grand Canyon**

1 Petroglyph Canyon, Valley of Fire

Petroglyph Canyon is the Valley of Fire's most popular attraction, carrying as it does the park's largest concentration of petroglyphs – primarily symbols incised by prehistoric Native Americans from the Lost City *(see below)*. The purpose of the petroglyphs is unclear: some may have been no more than the road signs of their day, while others might have had a religious or mystical significance. The trail goes to Mouse's Tank.
❧ *Map U2 • 702 397 2088 • Admission charge for park*

2 Lost City Museum of Archeology, Overton

Artifacts salvaged from Pueblo Grande de Nevada – now known as the Lost City – before it was inundated by Lake Mead are displayed at this pueblo-style museum. Exhibits include a reconstruction of the village, hunting weapons, and pottery.
❧ *721 S. Moapa Valley Blvd, Overton • Map U2 • 702 397 2193 • Open 8:30am–4:30pm daily • Admission charge*

3 Kolob Canyons, Zion National Park

The Kolob Canyons section offers viewpoints of steep canyons and a 5-mile (8-km) scenic drive. It also offers the closest access to Kolob Arch, which may be the largest free-standing arch in the world.
❧ *Map U1 • Information from Kolob Canyons Visitor Center, just east of exit 40 off I-15 north in Utah • 435 772 3256*

4 Zion Canyon

A shuttle system takes visitors along the scenic drive to the Temple of Sinawava (closed to private vehicles from April to October). Of special interest are the Court of the Patriarchs, the Streaked Wall, and the Virgin River. The Zion-Mt Carmel Highway is also a spectacular drive. If you can stay, head for Zion Lodge *(see also p107)*. Reserve a site early if you want to camp.
❧ *Map V1 • Information from Zion Canyon Visitor Center, Hwy 9, nr Springdale • 435 772 3256 • www.nps.gov/zion*

5 Bright Angel Point, North Rim, Grand Canyon

The North Rim of Grand Canyon may be more remote than the South Rim, but it is worth the effort. From the North Rim Visitor Center, walk the 0.25 mile (0.4 km) trail to Bright Angel Point for canyon views. ❧ *Map V2 • North Rim Visitor Center, Bright Angel Peninsula • Open mid-May–mid-Oct*

View from the North Rim

Following pages **Death Valley**

Left **Hopi House by Mary Colter, Grand Canyon** Right **Road to Mount Zion**

6 Yavapai Geology Museum, South Rim, Grand Canyon

For a visual introduction to Grand Canyon geology, you can scarcely beat the view from Yavapai Observation Station. Look down to the canyon floor for views of the Phantom Ranch and the Colorado River. The river flows along the bottom of the canyon, a little less than 5,000 ft (1,500 m) below the rim. From this great height it doesn't look very threatening, even with binoculars, but from the canyon floor it's a wildly impressive sight. ◈ *5 miles (8 km) N of south entrance • Map V2 • Open 8am–8pm*

7 The Watchtower, Desert View, Grand Canyon

A re-creation of an ancestral Puebloan tower, this landmark structure, designed by regional architect Mary Colter in 1932, is the highest point on the South Rim. The upper floor of the stone-built tower is decorated with Hopi murals. A gift store and refreshments are available. Other Colter designs at Grand Canyon include Hopi House, Hermits Rest, the Lookout Studio, and the cabins at Phantom Ranch. ◈ *On Hwy 64 at Desert View • Map V2*

Ancient Rocks

The Grand Canyon and Death Valley reveal more of the earth's geological history than anywhere else on the planet (some of its rocks are 1.7 billion years old). The mesas and cliffs of Zion National Park, too, were laid down and sculpted by the elements over millions of years. It is illegal to remove rocks or other artifacts from any national parks – if you do so, you may be fined.

8 Scotty's Castle, Death Valley

Less of a castle than a Mediterranean-style mansion, the main man-made visitor attraction at Death Valley was built in the 1920s by the Chicago insurance magnate Albert Johnson. But Wild West show cowboy and conman Walter Scott had a habit of bragging that the spread was his, and it came to be called Scotty's Castle after him. A nice twist to the tale is that, in his

Dante's View, Death Valley

Kolob Canyons

last years, Scott was befriended by Johnson and spent his final years at the coveted castle. Tours of the interior are available year round: fine craftsmanship is evident in the intricate wood carvings, wrought iron, and ornate tiling. It is possible to take a self-guided tour of the grounds. ◈ *Hwy 267, at N. end of Death Valley • Map S1 • 760 786 2392 • Grounds 7am–5:30pm daily, guided tours hourly • Admission fee*

9 Aguereberry Point, Death Valley

High in the Panamint Mountains, the point offers panoramic views across most of Death Valley, taking in Furnace Creek, the snowcapped Sierra Nevada, Devil's Golf Course, and other landmarks. The point is accessible by car down a long, rough 6.2-mile (10-km) gravel road, or by mountain bike, but excellent bike handling skills are needed for the climb. ◈ *Map S2 • Information from Furnace Creek Visitor Center • 760 786 3200 • Open 8am–5pm*

10 Dante's View, Death Valley

On the crest of the Black Mountains, this is one of the most spectacular overlooks in Death Valley. It is approximately 5,475 ft (1,668 m) above the Badwater salt flats – the lowest point in Death Valley – and is a wonderful place for watching the sunrise. The name was inspired by Dante's Inferno. ◈ *Dante's View Rd, 25 miles (40 km) S. of Furnace Creek • Map S2*

Three Trips from Vegas

Although it is possible to visit Zion, Grand Canyon, and Death Valley in one trip, it is not possible to do so in one day. Return to Las Vegas in between each place, making three separate excursions.

The Road to Zion

🕐 For an overnight trip to remember, drive east on Highway 15 to the Valley of Fire turning. Spend an hour or two on the park's scenic drive, hiking through **Petroglyph Canyon** *(see p99)* to Mouse's Tank and visiting the **Lost City Museum of Archeology** *(see p99)*. Then, back on Highway 15, proceed to Mesquite for lunch, making sure you are within reach of one of Zion's many viewpoints by sunset: you will be richly rewarded. Overnight in the park or at Springdale.

Grand Canyon

Take Highway 93 to Kingman, then Highways 40 and 64 to the national park. It is possible to view much of the canyon's grandeur by driving along the rim routes, but the total canyon experience involves hiking or riding to the valley floor, spending the night, and perhaps river-rafting. For insights into Native American culture, visit one of the reservations along the rim.

Death Valley

There are three major routes from Las Vegas to Death Valley. To choose the route most appropriate for your trip, visit www.nps.gov/deva for detailed information and planning tips. Light snacks and beverages are available for purchase from Scotty's Castle.

For more information on touring the region See p109

103

Left **Pinon trees** Center left **Iguana** Center right **Sagebrush** Right **Desert tortoise**

Top 10 Local Flora and Fauna

1 Pine Forests
Dense forests of scrubby piñon pine, stunted by poor, dry soil, grow 6,500 ft (2,000 m) above sea level in Grand Canyon (the canyon's highest elevation is 9,000 ft, or 2,750 m). About every seven years they produce bumper crops of edible nuts.

2 Wildflowers
Grand Canyon wildflowers include asters, sunflowers, globemallow, and Indian paintbrush. At Zion, look out for columbine, penstemon, Indian paint-brush, and many varieties of sunflowers. Death Valley has fewer species, but Panamint daisies grow in profusion.

3 Sagebrush
The Nevada state flower is found up to 10,000 ft (3,000 m) above sea level and grows as tall as seven feet (2 m). The dense clusters of tiny yellow or cream flowers bloom in late summer.

4 Birds of Prey
Red-tailed hawks are the most common predatory birds in all three parks, but at the Grand Canyon look out for the king of the skies, the golden eagle.

5 Tortoises
Two isolated populations of desert tortoise, the Mojave and the Sonoran, are found respect-ively in southern Utah and in the Grand Canyon, Death Valley, and other parts of the southwest.

6 Lizards
In Zion eastern fence lizards are among 13 local species, while chuckwallas, short-horned, and collared lizards all inhabit the Grand Canyon and Death Valley. Most common in Death Valley is the banded lizard.

Golden Eagle

7 Mountain Lions
These shy creatures roam the Grand Canyon, Zion, and the mountains around Death Valley. They generally eat larger mammals such as mule deer and bighorn sheep.

8 Deer
The unmistakable stiff-legged jump and large ears of the mule deer distinguish it through your binoculars from its graceful relative, the white-tail deer.

9 Snakes
Most species in the parks are harmless, but give rattlesnakes and sidewinders a wide berth.

10 Bears
Black bears are occasionally seen on the higher plateaus at Zion, but both they and grizzlies have long since disappeared from the Grand Canyon area, and no bears live in the mountains surrounding Death Valley or the Grand Canyon.

For desert precautions **See p133**

Left **Temple of Sinawava** Center **Panamint Mountains** Right **Great White Throne**

Natural Formations

1 Atlatl Rock, Valley of Fire
The most famous petroglyph here depicts an *atlatl*, a notched stick used to add speed and distance to a thrown spear. ◈ *Map U2*

2 Elephant Rock, Valley of Fire
Accessible via a short trail from the eastern entrance, this strange sandstone formation resembles an elephant's head – albeit with an oversize trunk. ◈ *Map U2*

3 Temple of Sinawava, Zion National Park
The temple is, in fact, an awe-inspiring mass of red rock. The religious name echoes many others in the park. ◈ *Map V1*

4 Great White Throne, Zion National Park
The sheer face of the Great White Throne, familiar to climbers worldwide, rises a staggering 2,200 ft (670 m) from the canyon floor, making it one of the world's tallest monoliths. ◈ *Map V1*

5 Kolob Arch, Zion National Park
Kolob Arch is too inaccessible to permit accurate measurements of its bulk, but it is thought to be as much as 230 ft high and 310 ft wide (70 m x 95 m). ◈ *Map V1*

6 Marble Canyon, Grand Canyon
The towering limestone walls have given the upper section of the Grand Canyon its name. ◈ *Map V2*

7 Inner Gorge, Grand Canyon
Sheer granite cliffs drop 1,000 feet (300 m) to the canyon floor to form this vertiginous gorge. Two nerve-testing suspension bridges make the crossing near Phantom Ranch. ◈ *Map V2*

8 San Francisco Mountains, Grand Canyon
Named the "Kingdom of St. Francis" by explorer Marcos de Niza, the range rises to an impressive 12,655 ft (3,857 m), the highest point in the state of Arizona. ◈ *Map V2*

9 Funeral Mountains, Death Valley
A geological fault line was responsible for tilting these spectacular mountains on their sides. ◈ *Map S1*

10 Panamint Mountains, Death Valley
The Panamint Mountains are one of five mountain ranges in Death Valley. Head for Aguereberry Point for amazing views of the Funeral Mountains and the Sierra Nevada beyond. ◈ *Map S2*

Funeral Mountains

 For more on the Grand Canyon **See pp16–19**

Price Categories
For a three course
meal for one with a
half bottle of wine (or
equivalent meal), taxes
and extra charges.

$	under $20
$$	$20–$30
$$$	$30–$45
$$$$	$45–$60
$$$$$	over $60

Left **Thunderbird, Mt Carmel** Right **Flanigan's Café, Zion**

TOP 10 Places to Eat

1 El Tovar Dining Room, Grand Canyon
The room is built of pine logs and stone and features fine china, crystal, and linen-covered tables. Fresh seafood is flown in daily, and the veal dishes are excellent. ◈ El Tovar Hotel, South Rim • Map V2 • 928 638 2631 • $$$$

El Tovar Dining Room

2 Coronado Room, Grand Canyon
Prime rib, chicken marsala, and stuffed trout are favorites at this Spanish-style eatery. ◈ Best Western Squire Inn, Tusayan • Map V2 • 928 638 2681 • $$$

3 Bright Angel Lodge Restaurant, Grand Canyon
Hearty Southwest American fare. ◈ Bright Angel Lodge • Map V2 • 928 638 2631 • $$

4 Arizona Room, Grand Canyon
A Southwest decor in muted pastels is the setting for the all-American favorite of big steaks, baked potatoes, and crisp salads. ◈ Bright Angel Lodge • Map V2 • 928 638 2631 • $$$

5 Maswik Lodge Cafeteria, Grand Canyon
Wholesome food at reasonable prices. For a pre- or post-meal drink, the lodge includes a sports bar with wide-screen TV. ◈ Map V2 • Maswik Lodge • 303 297 2757 • $$

6 The Spotted Dog Café, Zion
Among the house specialties are salads, pasta, red trout, chicken, Utah lamb, and Black Angus beef. ◈ Springdale • Map U1 • 435 772 3244 • Open for dinner only • $$$

7 Picnic Areas, Zion Canyon and Springdale
Buy picnic provisions at Oscar's Deli and a bumbleberry pie at the Bumbleberry Restaurant in Springdale for an al fresco meal in a nearby picnic area. ◈ Map U1 • $$

8 East Zion Thunderbird Lodge Restaurant, Mt Carmel
American fare in a family dining room, where the pies, breads, and sweet rolls are home-made. ◈ Mt Carmel Jtn • Map U1 • 435 648 2203 • $$

9 The Inn at Furnace Creek Dining Room, Death Valley
Elegant dining room with lace tablecloths, firelight flickering on the adobe walls, and views of the Panamint Mountains. Continental fare is served from a varied à la carte menu. Open mid-October to mid-May. ◈ Furnace Creek Inn • Map S1 • 760 786 2345 • $$$$$

10 Stovepipe Wells Village, Death Valley
The Toll Road Restaurant offers eclectic fare all year long. ◈ Stovepipe Wells • Map S2 • 760 786 2387 • $$

Price Categories

For a standard,	**$**	under $50
double room per	**$$**	$50–$100
night (with breakfast	**$$$**	$100–$150
if included), taxes,	**$$$$**	$150–$200
and extra charges.	**$$$$$**	over $200

Left **Best Western Zion Park Inn** Right **Furnace Creek Inn**

🔟 Places to Stay

1 Best Western Squire Inn, Grand Canyon
The 250-room inn has its own tennis court, heated pool, sauna, billiards, video games, beauty salon, and bowling alley. 🅢 *100 Arizona 64 • Map V2 • 928 638 2681 • $$$*

2 El Tovar Hotel, Grand Canyon
Historic hotel built by pioneer resort builders, the Fred Harvey Company, in 1905. It is patterned after the great hunting lodges of Europe with a stone fireplace and mounted animals. 🅢 *South Rim • Map V2 • 928 638 2631 • $$$$*

3 Grand Canyon Lodge
The only hotel accommodation on the North Rim of the canyon, this lodge has cabins and a few modern motel rooms. Advance reservations are essential. 🅢 *Bright Angel Point • Map V2 • 303 297 2757 • www.grandcanyonlodges.com • $$$*

4 Camper Village
With 250 RV hook-ups and 100 tent sites, this is one of the larger, privately run, year-round campgrounds. 🅢 *Tusayan • Map V2 • 928 638 2887 • $*

5 Zion Lodge
The complex includes 40 cabins with gas log fireplaces and private porches, and 80 rooms, each with two queen-size beds. 🅢 *Zion National Park • Map U1 • 435 772 7700 • $$$$*

6 Best Western Zion Park Inn
Located at the foot of The Watchman, the 120 rooms here are individually climate-controlled and some have kitchenettes. 🅢 *1215 Zion Park Blvd, Springdale • Map U1 • 800 934 7275, 435 772 3200 • $$$*

7 Cliffrose Lodge & Gardens, Zion
The setting is charming, with five acres of lawns, shade trees, and flower gardens along the Virgin River. Every room offers a spectacular view. 🅢 *281 Zion Park Blvd, Springdale • Map U1 • 435 772 3234 • $$$*

8 Furnace Creek Inn, Death Valley
Elegant and expensive, with glorious views of the Panamint Mountains. Guest rooms have quality furnishings. Open mid-October to mid-May. 🅢 *Furnace Creek • Map S1 • 760 786 2345 • $$$$$*

9 Furnace Creek Ranch, Death Valley
The rustic hostelry offers two spring-fed pools (the water is very warm), golf, tennis, and horseback riding. 🅢 *Furnace Creek • Map S1 • 760 786 2361 • $$$*

10 Stovepipe Wells Village, Death Valley
A bit off the beaten track, this is not a fancy place but has a pool, saloon, and general store. The nearby sand dunes are a photographer's delight. 🅢 *Stovepipe Wells • Map S2 • 760 786 2387 • $$$*

Left **Hikers** Center left **Lake Mead marina** Center right **Sign on desert road**

Hiking Trails

1 Mouse's Tank, Valley of Fire
"Mouse" was the name of a Native American outlaw. The moderately easy trail to Mouse's Tank (a series of natural catchments) passes the best petroglyphs in the park.

2 Canyon Overlook Trail, Zion National Park
A moderate, short day-hike to the overlook, with great views of lower Zion Canyon.

3 Observation Point Trail Zion
The 8-mile (12.9-km) round-trip hike is moderately difficult to Hidden Canyon, then strenuous to Observation Point. There is a 2,148-ft (655-m) elevation gain.

4 Riverside Walk, Zion
The paved walk at the base of a gorge is especially delightful in early November when the fall foliage is at its most beautiful.

5 Bright Angel Trail, Grand Canyon
The entire 19-mile (30-km)

Kilns, Wildrose Canyon

down-and-back round-trip descends 4,400 ft (1,342 m) and takes most hikers two days. Rest houses and a campground are on the route. Backcountry permits are required for overnight trips.

6 Rim Trail, Grand Canyon
Extending from the Village area, the partially paved trail can be accessed at many points along Hermit Road and its terminus at the South Kaibab trailhead. There is little elevation change and great views.

7 South Kaibab Trail, Grand Canyon
Access to the trailhead is by shuttle bus. The steep trail descends 4,500 ft (1,372 m), with no water along the down-and-back 14-mile (22-km) route.

8 Wildrose Canyon to Wildrose Peak, Death Valley
A 4-mile (6-km) climb through woodland to the crest of the Panamint Mountains. Superb views.

9 Golden Canyon to Zabriskie Point, Death Valley
A low-elevation, 6-mile (9.5-km) round-trip hike, traversing an area of fully exposed rock strata that represents millions of years.

10 Coffin Peak Trail, Death Valley
This easy trail starts at Dante's View, following a canyon into the Black Mountains. Vegetation is dominated by spiny desert shrubs.

Left **All-terrain vehicle** Center **Start of scenic route** Right **Mountain biker**

🔟 Commercial Tours

1 GC Flight
This company runs helicopter and airplane flights, as well as motor coach tours from Las Vegas to the Grand Canyon and Hoover Dam. Flights can also be taken over the Strip. ☏ 702 629 7776 • www.gcflight.com

2 Papillon Grand Canyon Helicopters
The Grand Celebration Tour includes landing on the floor of the Grand Canyon, a champagne picnic, and views of Lake Mead and Hoover Dam. Other add-ons are available. ☏ 702 736 7243 • www.papillon.com

3 Awesome Adventures
Several tour options include the desert, Lake Mead, and in the Valley of Fire. Lunch and hotel pick-up are included. ☏ 888 846 4747 • www.awesome adventures.com

4 Grand Canyon Express
Grand Canyon Express offers standard air, boat, and motor coach tours as well as VIP options. ☏ 800 843 8724 • www.airvegas.com

5 Canyon Explorations
One of several companies providing hiking, interpretive trips, and whitewater rafting in the Grand Canyon. ☏ 928 774 4559

6 ATV Wilderness Tours
Year-round guided trips in four-wheel all-terrain vehicles and jeeps. Three- to six-hour outings are available. The company is based in St. George, Utah. ☏ 888 656 2887 • www.atvadventures.com

7 Adventure Photo Tours
Full- and half-day tours hit the highlights so visitors can capture ghost towns, wild horses, petroglyphs, old mines, sandstone formations, and wild-flowers on camera. ☏ 888 363 8687 • www.adventurephototours.com

8 Pink Jeep Tours
Known for its knowledgeable guides, Pink Jeep offers several half- and full-day tours in the area. Tours are conducted in 10-person trekkers, so groups are kept to a manageable size. It is also one of the few tour companies with off-road permits. ☏ 888 900 4480 • www.pinkjeeptours.com

9 Tickets and Tours
Hoover Dam day trips are offered, along with tours of the Grand Canyon and Red Rock Canyon. More obscure excursions, such as a champagne night tour of Haunted Vegas, are also offered. ☏ 800 838 8155, 702 617 5513 • lasvegas.showtickets.com

10 Zion Ponderosa Ranch Resort
A number of guided activities, such as hiking, abseiling, mountain biking, and horseback riding just outside Zion National Park. ☏ 435 648 2700 • www.zion ponderosa.com

Following pages **New York-New York Hotel, Las Vegas**

STREETSMART

LAS VEGAS TOP 10

Left **Golfing holiday** Right **Summer sun**

TOP 10 What to Pack and When to Go

1 Rate Changes
Hotel rates skyrocket when the weather is best – from about mid-March through July and September until the first part of November. However, days can be close to perfect during February and November when rates are generally lower and there is less traffic and smaller crowds. Las Vegas casino hotels offer lower rates on weekdays, with rates soaring on weekends and during conventions.

2 Tee-Timing
It's easier for golfers to get tee times from November to March. Although it can be windy, the temperature is usually comfortable for playing. In the summer, book tee times in the early morning before it gets too hot.

3 Consider Convention Dates
The three biggest annual conventions in Las Vegas, in January, April, and November, each attract well over 100,000 delegates. Do your utmost not to coincide with them: not only will room rates be at their highest, but traffic is heavy, and the lines waiting for restaurant service can be daunting.

4 Daytime Wear
As far as clothes are concerned, just about anything goes. Although shorts and T-shirts are the uniform in very hot weather, you'll see people wearing everything from designer resort wear to jeans and leather jackets the rest of the year. Bathing attire should be reserved for swimming pool areas. Women wear cover-ups and men generally wear shirts and shorts over their bathing suits when going between their rooms and the pool. Upscale hotels provide robes for guests' use.

5 After Dark Apparel
While comfort generally rules the dress code, some moderately priced restaurants have signs saying "No shoes, no shirts, no service." Sport coats (casual-styled jackets) are required at some of the more expensive restaurants, but neckties are not always a requisite. Most people dress up when going to production shows or nightclubs; Las Vegas residents tend to dress more formally (and flamboyantly) than visitors.

6 Health Matters
The sun shines an average of more than 300 days a year, so pack sunglasses, sunscreen, moisturizer, and a hat.

7 Weather Wise
Keep in mind more than just the glorious sunshine: Las Vegas receives an average of only 4.2 inches of rainfall a year, with about half an inch falling during the wettest months, January and August. The average humidity is 30.1 percent, but it can feel drier. Winter is unpredictable: some days are cold and windy, while others are warm enough for wearing shorts.

8 US Entry Requirements for Canadian Visitors
Canadians do need passports, and must show a photo I.D., such as a citizenship card, when entering the USA.

9 US Entry Requirements for Overseas Visitors
Citizens from Australia, New Zealand, Japan, Germany, France, the UK, and many other European countries can visit the USA for up to 90 days without a visa, so long as they have a valid passport. They will need to register and pay a fee at https://esta.cbp.dhs.gov prior to departure. Visitors from countries who do need a visa must apply to a US consulate or embassy, and may be asked for evidence of financial solvency and proof that they intend to return to their country of origin.

10 US Customs
Adult nonresidents are permitted to bring in a limited amount of duty-free goods. These include 0.2 gallons (1 liter) of alcohol, 200 cigarettes, 50 cigars (but not Cuban), and up to $100 worth of gifts. Cash amounts over $10,000 should be declared.

For advice on health and things to avoid See pp131–3

Left **McCarran International Airport** Center **Car-rental agency** Right **Fly-drive option**

🔟 Arriving in Las Vegas

1 Air News
If you're one of the millions of people who fly to McCarran International Airport, check out the airport website for information and maps. It is one of the busiest airports in the USA and can be a bit confusing, especially in the early mornings and on weekends.

2 Comparison Shopping
McCarran is served by all major US carriers and several international carriers, including Virgin Atlantic and British Airways, with both scheduled and charter flights.

3 Fly-Drive and Gambling Deals
Fly-drive packages are a firm favorite with people on vacation in the USA. "Gamblers' Specials" combine air travel and accommodation in Las Vegas.

4 Getting from the Airport to the City
The airport is 2.5 miles (4 km) south of the city center. Allow 10 minutes to travel by road between the airport and hotels on the Strip. Taxis, shuttles, and limousines wait outside the airport, and there are car rental agencies inside. The cheapest option is a bus: the RTC (Regional Transportation Commission) bus routes WAX 108 and 109 run between the airport, downtown, and the Strip.

5 Paying Fares
If you have forgotten to bring enough change for transportation between the airport and your hotel, cash machines (ATMs) are located throughout the airport, and these accept standard cards such as Visa, MasterCard, and American Express, as well as other major US cards.

6 Car Rental
If you are renting a car from the airport, be advised that the rental price may not include three taxes, which total nearly 30 percent, charged on all airport car rentals. If you are in a hurry, use one of the rental agencies with counters at the airport, but bear in mind that agencies with off-site counters generally charge lower rates.

7 Car Rental Documents
Visitors who plan to rent a car must have a valid driver's license and major credit card, both of which are required by all agencies. Drivers who are at least 25 years old can rent a car. Those who are aged between 21 and 24 may be able to rent one for an additional charge. If your own automobile insurance does not cover rental vehicles, it is wise to buy the rental companies' own coverage.

Directory

Air News
www.mccarran.com

8 Road Rules
Visitors from abroad who plan to rent automobiles would be well advised to familiarize themselves with basic US driving rules and signage before they begin driving. Information is available at most vehicle-rental agencies.

9 Arriving by Road
If you are driving to Las Vegas from another part of the USA, you'll probably access the city either via I-15, which goes from Los Angeles to Salt Lake City, Utah, and beyond, or via I-95, which connects Washington, Oregon, Nevada, and Arizona. Try to avoid peak traffic times on these roads: busiest periods are 7–9am and 4–7pm.

10 Arriving by Train and Bus
Visitors who wish to travel to Las Vegas by train and bus can take the Amtrak Chief to Los Angeles then transfer to the Amtrak bus service, which arrives at the Las Vegas Greyhound Station. For timetable and ticket information telephone 1 800 872 7245 or visit www.amtrak.com.

For more on booking accommodations **See p135**

Left **Las Vegas monorail** Right **Local taxi**

🔟 Getting Around

Foot Power
Walking may well be the best way to travel the 4-mile (6-inch) long Strip: the sidewalks are wide and the terrain is flat. Since the city covers a large area, however, and is crisscrossed by multi-lane streets, you'll need a car or public transportation when visiting attractions in outlying areas. Carry plenty of water if you plan to walk anywhere; never forget you're in the desert!

Finding Your Routes
If you are going to be driving, procure a good map (the Rand McNally map, which can be obtained at supermarkets, drugstores, and booksellers, is excellent). The city is laid out on a grid, with only a few principal thoroughfares running obliquely. An up-to-date GPS system can also be a helpful tool if you are driving.

Traffic Talk
In town, be prepared for fast driving and heavy traffic. Avoid driving during rush hours (about 7–9am and 4–7pm). Congestion on the Strip begins in late morning and continues until after midnight, especially on weekends from mid-March through October and when large special events take place. The city's major streets are six to eight lanes wide.

Parking Lots and Garages
Hotel-casinos on the Strip provide free parking in high-rise garages, although some in downtown require ticket validation for free parking. Almost all hotels offer valet parking. When valet parking is full, be aware that preference is always given to hotel guests over casino visitors.

On-street Parking
When parking on the street, be sure to read all posted signs about parking restrictions to avoid incurring fines or having your vehicle towed away. Fines for parking in disability-reserved spaces without a valid placard start at $250.

Taxis
Hotel entrances on the Strip and downtown are the best places to find cabs. The standard fare includes an initial fee of $3.30, plus $2.60 for each additional mile, and about $0.25 a minute when stopped at a red light or stalled in traffic. In heavy traffic, it can cost more than $20 to go from one end of the Strip to the other. Since taxi drivers know the city's less-busy streets, a useful tip is to ask to be taken the quickest way rather than the shortest.

Trams and Monorail
Free trams connect TI with the Mirage and the Excalibur with Luxor and Mandalay Bay. There is also a tram that runs from the Bellagio and Monte Carlo to Crystals at City-Center. The monorail operates along the Strip between MGM Grand and Sahara (7am–2am Mon–Thu, 7am–3am Fri–Sun). A one-ride ticket costs $5.

Public Transit System
The least-expensive way to travel beyond downtown and the Strip is by the bus system run by the Regional Transportation Commission (RTC). There is an extensive network of routes. Deuce and Strip & Downtown Express lines run along the Strip. A 24-hour pass on the Strip and downtown buses cost $8. A 2-hour pass is $6.

Hotel Shuttles
You may have to pay for the shuttle service between the airport and some hotels, but others offer a free service to shopping areas and sightseeing destinations.

Bike Riding
Bicycling along main arteries is not advised, but riding through residential neighborhoods and at Red Rock Canyon, away from the hubbub, can be nice. Bikes can be rented from various outlets; fees usually include helmets.

Left **Ace Gold bus** Right **Vegas-style private tour vehicles**

TOP10 Sources of Information

1 General Information

For overall information about the city, including accommodations, attractions, and shopping, contact the Las Vegas Convention & Visitors Authority (LVCVA).

2 Business Information

Visitors interested in business in the area can contact the Las Vegas Chamber of Commerce, which will direct them to the appropriate sources.

Directory

Regional Transportation Commission
702 228 7433

Las Vegas Convention & Visitors Authority
3150 Paradise Rd • 702 892 0711 • www. lasvegas.com

Las Vegas Chamber of Commerce
8363 W. Sunset Rd • 702 641 5822

Asian Chamber of Commerce
6272 Spring Mountain Rd • 702 737 4300

Urban Chamber of Commerce
1951 Stella Lake St • 702 648 6222

Latin Chamber of Commerce
300 N. 13th St • 702 385 7367

Las Vegas Advisor
3665 S. Procyon Ave • 702 252 0655

3 Ethnic Affairs

Information about Las Vegas's various ethnic businesses and attractions is available from such organizations as the Asian Chamber of Commerce, Black Chamber of Commerce, and Latin Chamber of Commerce.

4 Organization Information

If you belong to a worldwide organization such as Rotary International or would like to meet people with similar vocational interests or hobbies, your best source of information is an Internet search engine such as www.google.com or www.yahoo.com.

5 Magazine Information

For insights into places and people, pick up *What's On*, a bimonthly magazine, or *Where*, a monthly publication, aimed at visitors. Both are available in tourist areas and visitor centers. They contain articles as well as information on nightlife, shopping, gaming, and attractions.

6 Newspaper News

The *Las Vegas Review Journal* publishes dining and entertainment news throughout the week, as well as a "Best of Las Vegas" section once a year in March.

You'll learn a lot by reading the ads, too!

7 Internet Info

For information on airlines, rental cars, and accommodations, use your favorite search engine to find websites with a Las Vegas focus. One of the most useful sites of the many available is www. lasvegas.com.

8 Cost Cutting

Bargain hunters should pick up coupon books available throughout the resorts and check hotel websites directly for discounts on accommodation, dining, and attractions.

9 Tourist Stations

The tourist stations along the Strip not only sell commercial tours, but they also have display racks containing promotional material about various attractions, which may be of use to you.

10 Out-of-Town Source

People traveling to Las Vegas via I-15 manage to find special offers and deals that don't seem to be advertised anywhere else: the tourist information center in Jean, Nevada (near the border with California) has a reputation for handling the best Las Vegas coupons.

Left **Bellagio's shopping arcade** Center **A Vegas shopping mall** Right **Pawnshop**

TOP 10 Shopping Tips

1 Shopping Arcades
Count on finding the most interesting upscale shopping in hotel arcades such as Miracle Mile Shops at Planet Holly-wood (see p52), Bellagio's Via Bellagio (see pp14–15), and The Forum Shops at Caesars Palace (see pp26–7). All these are on Las Vegas Boule-vard South, otherwise known as the Strip.

2 Malls
You have several choices for major mall-hopping. Boulevard, Meadows, and the Galleria at Sunset (see p52) are patronized primarily by locals, while tourists form the majority at two upscale malls on the Strip – The Forum Shops at Caesars (see pp26–7) and Fashion Show (see p52). The best sales at upscale shops such as Nieman Marcus and Saks Fifth Avenue (both at Fashion Show) are held in January.

3 Bargain Buys
For bargains in high-quality merchandise, seek out the outlet centers. Las Vegas Premium Outlets (see pp53 & 91) are located just a few minutes south of the Strip, and on Charleston Boulevard at the north end. The dozens of brands featured here include 7 For All Man-kind, American Apparel, Banana Republic Factory Store, DKNY, Elie Tahari,

Juicy Couture, and Nike Factory Store. It is especially worth visiting these stores at the end of summer, when the merchandise is marked down even further.

4 Antiques
There are several antique and vintage clothing shops located in Downtown Las Vegas. If you have time to visit only one, however, go to Antique Mall of America (see p91) where dozens of dealers sell goods. Some of the interesting items for sale include comics, costume jewelry, cloth-ing, kitchen and house-ware items, coins, Asian art, and toys. There's ample parking too.

5 Ethnic Shops
For the best authentic ethnic shopping, go to the stores that serve Las Vegas' various ethnic populations such as Asian Market (953 E. Sahara), Cardenas Market (4700 Meadows Ln), International Marketplace (5000 S. Decatur Blvd), Marlana's Supermarket (3631 W. Sahara Ave), and those in Chinatown Plaza (see p85 & 91).

6 Swap Meets
Swap meets, or flea markets, are usually held on Friday, Saturday, and Sunday, and are a great place to browse for bargains. The biggest

meets are Fantastic Indoor Swap Meet (see p91) and Broadacres Marketplace & Event Center (see p85).

7 Pawn Shops
If you've never visited a pawn shop, Las Vegas is your chance. Much of the merchandise comes, of course, from gamblers in search of that little bit more money. There are several pawn shops located downtown, the most well-known and popular of which is Gold & Silver Pawn (see p80). If you want to make a purchase, don't agree to pay the first price you're quoted. Maybe not the second or third, either!

8 Business Hours
The larger malls and arcades are generally open 10am–9pm, seven days a week. Elsewhere, stores may be closed on Sunday. Some of the Forum Shops at Caesars stay open until midnight.

9 Taxes
Clark County levies an 8.1 percent "sales and use" tax on most goods. This is added to purchases at the cash register.

10 Credit Cards
Most businesses accept Visa and Master-Card. American Express, Diners, and other cards are not accepted as widely; travelers' checks in US dollars are accept-ed at many stores.

 For more on shopping and souvenirs **See pp52–5, 83 & 91**

Left **Buffet restaurant** Center **The Convention Center** Right **The Mirage Volcano**

🔟 Ways to Save Money

1 Planning Ahead
Start planning early – the best airfares may require three months' advance purchase.

2 Airline Deals from Other Parts of the USA
Combined air and hotel packages from most US cities to Las Vegas are especially good bargains. Keep in mind that airline fares to hub cities served by a number of carriers are almost always less expensive than routes on which there are few competing airlines.

3 Airline Deals from Other Countries
When Las Vegas is among two or more destinations you plan to visit in the USA, price each segment of your trip's airfare separately. Visitors from Europe, for example, often save money by buying round-trip tickets from their home country to New York or Chicago and then traveling in the USA by using a combination of one-way bargain air tickets and rental cars.

4 Timing
Time your trip to save money. Hotel rates change from day to day, based on supply and demand. They're most expensive on weekends, holidays, and during big conventions and important events.

The less restricted your travel dates, the more money you can save: a room that costs $300 a night on a busy May weekend can go for $110 in November. Airfares are usually lower during the winter months, too.

5 Car Rentals
Car-rental rates change even more rapidly – sometimes hourly. Shop around online for the best deal, and call rental companies directly to inquire about special offers. Most companies require a credit card deposit.

6 Freebie Sources
When you arrive in the city, go directly to the information center run by the Las Vegas Convention & Visitors Authority (see p115). Collect all the free magazines and brochures you can comfortably carry. Inside are coupons for special offers and money off shows and dinners, etc.

7 Meal Cost-Cutting
Eat your big meal of the day at noon. Lunch buffets usually cost a few dollars less than those offered at night, with virtually the same food served at both. If you're an early bird or a night owl, you'll save money on food: several casinos – notably those downtown and in outlying areas – offer low-cost

meals between 11pm and 6 or 7am. These also work well for visitors affected by jet lag.

8 Discount Shopping
If you want to save money traveling to and from the stores on the Strip, and downtown, buy an $8 24-hour pass for easy access on the Deuce and Strip & Downtown Express buses.

9 Entertainment Savings
The extravagant nightly light-and-sound shows and street performances at the Fremont Street Experience (see p79) are all free. Many of the big hotels along the Strip put on spectacular free shows to entice people in (see p76). There are also less well-publicized free attractions, such as the Flamingo Wildife Habitat (see p67) which has more than 300 birds. People-watching is entertaining, too (see p77).

10 Free Special Events
Every so often, casinos put on promotions, bands present concerts, and organizations sponsor other free events. These are listed in the calendar sections of local papers and the various free-entertainment magazines. Fremont Street is a hotspot for free concerts and events, so head there for guaranteed entertainment.

Left *The Mirage* dolphin habitat Center *Excalibur* Right *Cirque du Soleil* at Bellagio

Types of Entertainment

1 Production Shows

Plan to see at least one production show (long-running show with spectacular production effects) while you're in town. A Las Vegas visit simply isn't complete without experiencing the excitement and profess-ionalism of these top-notch performances. Although shows such as *"O"* and *Celine Dion* are expensive, others that cost less than half of their prices are also very well done.

2 Showtime

Most big shows go on twice nightly, with one or two nights off a week (varying from show to show). Each show also has a few weeks off every year, so check schedules in advance. Daytime shows usually cost less.

3 Dining Options

Although most shows don't include meals or cocktails (there are refreshment stands outside most theaters), some hotels still feature dinner and cocktail shows. If you can, opt for the cocktail shows: they're less expensive. Dinner shows offer a fun 2-in-1 option.

4 Other Shows

The production spectaculars aren't the only shows in town. Other long-running shows in hotel/casino theaters star magicians, comedians, and impersonators. Comedians on their way up also appear on Las Vegas comedy club stages.

5 Headliner Shows

If you're determined to see a particular entertainer perform in one of the city's famous headliner extravaganzas, order your tickets as soon as you hear about the performance. If you hesitate, you will prob-ably still be able to buy tickets, but they will most likely be for the poorest seats in the priciest category. Las Vegas is a venue where top entertainers typically present just one perfor-mance; while the least expensive tickets may cost less than $100, top tickets can cost more than $1,000.

6 Lounge Shows

To stretch your entertain-ment dollars, take in a lounge show or two. This is where the new-est, potentially next big acts are found. You can watch some lounge acts for the price of a drink. Others are free.

7 Piano Lounges

In a number of piano lounges around Las Vegas, professional players accept tips to play your favourite tunes.

8 Chance Entertainment

In a town where entertainment is the name of the game, most Las Vegas visitors happen upon some unexpected treat during their visit. It may be a Dixieland band playing in a hotel plaza, a dance recital at a shopping center, a string quartet playing in a park, or strolling entertainers at the theme hotels.

9 Adults Only

Several clubs in the area around West Sahara Street south of down-town present adult-only entertainment. With names like Crazy Horse Saloon, Sapphire, and Palomino Club, they feature topless or nude waitresses, amateur strip contests, and "beautiful friendly hostess dancers."

10 Culture

High culture doesn't necessarily come to mind when one thinks of Las Vegas. It is, in fact, the city's best-kept entertain-ment secret. Top-drawer artists from around the world perfom regularly here: Luciano Pavarotti sang at the Mandalay Bay; top orchestras and ballet troupes can be seen at the university. In addition, performers in the Las Vegas shows take part in actors equity, ballet, and musical productions when not in their regular roles.

Left *Jubilee!* Center *Le Rêve – The Dream* Right *KÁ*

TOP 10 Tips on Buying Tickets

1 Advance Bookings
To avoid disappointment, order tickets for any production shows you want to see well in advance. You can do this either through your travel agent, by contacting the box office directly (when the production is at a hotel/casino theater, you can phone the hotel and your call will be transferred), or through a ticket agency such as Ticketmaster. It is almost impossible for ordinary tourists to buy tickets to the top shows such as *"O"* and *Mystère* on the day of the performance even if they are staying in the hotel where the show is playing.

2 Discount Tickets
Surplus same-day tickets for shows are sold at a discount at Tix4Tonight at Hawaiian Marketplace, outside Fashion Show Mall, just south of the Riviera, the Four Queens hotel, and near the giant Coke bottle north of MGM Grand.

3 Standby
When you want to see a show and can't get tickets in advance, you will increase your chances of getting standby seats by arriving early so you get one of the first places in line.

4 VIPs
If you're a high roller, you probably won't have to worry about standing in line at shows or anywhere else. Just let the VIP desk know what you would like to see. VIP packages are usually sold for most shows, and combine great seats with meals and drinks.

5 Charting Your Course
When it is possible, ask to see the theater's seating chart. It's probably true that in many theaters there isn't a bad seat in the house. Still, some seats are better than others, and as long as they all cost the same price, it is worthwhile choosing the ones you want.

6 Tipping
Tipping the *maître d'* or usher isn't always necessary. A growing number of theater tickets are issued electronically, and your seat is determined before you enter the theater. If you have VIP seats, or an usher goes out of his way to show you to a better seat, however, it may be appropriate to tip a few dollars.

7 Box Offices
Guests can buy tickets online for almost all shows, and they'll need to pick them up prior to the performance. Note when tickets should be picked up (usually one hour before curtain) as they may be resold if you are late.

8 Other Cultural Venues
Tickets for cultural programs presented at such venues as community arts centers and outdoor amphitheaters are usually, but not always, available from commercial ticket agencies including Ticketmaster. Several websites list all available shows on any given day or at any given location.

9 Tour Group Tickets
People who are interested primarily in seeing Las Vegas shows should consult with their travel agents about tours that include them in their itineraries.

10 Ticket Information
In most cases, you should be able to buy tickets directly from the specific venue. If the venue isn't selling tickets, inquire anyway as staff will know who to contact in order to secure them.

Directory
Ticketmaster
800 745 3000

119

Left **Getting married at Bellagio** Center **Wedding chapel** Right **Elvis Presley's Vegas wedding**

Getting Married in Las Vegas

Getting a License
Marriage license requirements in Nevada have traditionally been less stringent than those in other parts of the USA. No blood tests are needed, nor is it necessary, after the license has been issued, to wait a set period before getting married. To obtain a marriage license, both partners must appear at the County Clerk's office in the Clark County Courthouse. Well over 100,000 weddings are performed in Clark County each year.

Identity Proof
Be prepared to produce your social security number and proof of identity such as a driver's license, certified copy of birth certificate, passport, or military ID. Divorced

applicants need evidence that their divorces have been finalized, including date, city, and state where the decree was granted.

Age of Consent
People aged 18 years and older do not need consent to get married, but those aged between 16 and 18 must either have a consenting parent present or else produce a notorized document from a parent giving his or her consent.

Time-Saver
Couples planning a St. Valentine's Day or New Year's Eve wedding should get their licenses well in advance to avoid long lines at the County Clerk's office.

Wedding Officiants
Nevada law requires that couples be married by civil marriage commissioners, justices of the peace, or bona fide ministers.

Civil Ceremonies
Civil marriages are performed one block from the Courthouse in The Office of Civil Marriages, for a fee of $75 in cash or by credit card. One witness is required in addition to the person performing the ceremony.

Religious Rules
If your decision to have a religious wedding in Las Vegas is not a spur of the moment one, then have your usual minister,

priest, or rabbi contact the head of the church or synagogue in Las Vegas where you want the ceremony to be held. That way you can resolve any discrepancies that may exist between different denominations regarding preparation for marriage, publication of banns, and the like.

Prices
You need $60 – in cash – for the license. Budget $75 for the use of a wedding chapel in a no-frills ceremony, $50 for the minister, plus any flowers, music, or costume rental. Weddings featuring an Elvis impersonator as minister start at $200. Make arrangements for a wedding-chapel ceremony in advance: they can't oblige drop-ins when fully booked.

Venues
With more than four dozen chapels, hundreds of churches, synagogues, public parks, ballrooms, and scenic spots, the number of wedding venues is limited only by the imagination; some officiants may be unwilling to perform skydiving or helicopter ceremonies!

Same-Sex Ceremonies
Same-sex marriages are not recognized in Nevada, but the Gay Chapel of Las Vegas, part of Viva Las Vegas Wedding Chapel (see p50), performs commitment ceremonies.

Directory

Clark County Marriage License Bureau
201 E. Clark Ave
• Open 8am–midnight daily • 702 671 0500

Commissioner of Civil Marriages
309 S. 3rd St • 2–6pm Mon–Thu, 10am–9pm Fri, 12:30–9pm Sun

Purple Unions (gay weddings)
www.purpleunions.com/usa/nevada.html

Left **Little Church of the West** Center **Wedding chapel** Right **Romantic Pamplemousse**

TOP 10 Honeymoon Packages

Hotel Packages
Since honeymoon packages are offered by virtually all of the hotels in Las Vegas, it definitely pays to shop around. The basic packages usually include an upgraded room, a bottle of champagne with souvenir champagne flutes, optional breakfast in bed, and dinner at one of the hotel's restaurants.

Seasonal Price Variations
Whereas wedding licenses cost $60 year-round and chapel fees remain fairly constant (St. Valentine's Day and New Year's Eve being exceptions), honeymoon package prices are affected by the dates you choose. For example, a week-long honeymoon during any major conventions in the city may well cost two to four times what it might during the preceding or following week.

Bed-and-Breakfast Packages
If you fancy getting away from the crowds and bright lights, investigate bed-and-breakfast honeymoon packages and houseboat rentals for a more relaxed stay. (See also page 134.)

Internet Deals
Explore your options on the Internet. All Las Vegas hotels have websites. Most of these include information on package deals.

Do-It-Yourself
You may feel that rather than opt for a lavish package you can make your honeymoon more special by doing it yourself, finding a regular hotel package (or booking a romantic suite on the Strip) and adding your own romantic touches – a box of Ethel M gourmet chocolates (produced in Las Vegas), dining at an intimate restaurant such as Pamplemousse (see p46) and seeing the shows you choose.

Accommodation Advice
As far as accommodations are concerned, the general rule is that the further away you are from the Strip, the less expensive the rooms. There are, however, deluxe exceptions to the rule, such as the classy Green Valley Ranch, Red Rock Casino Resort, and JW Marriott Las Vegas.

Professional Planning
For those who would rather not plan the details, most resorts have professional wedding planners and packages; contact them directly.

Trousseau Tip
Save some of your trousseau money for lingerie shopping in Las Vegas. The little nothings sold at places like Bare Essentials and Bad Attitude Boutique are definitely unusual!

Wedding Photos
For an inexpensive souvenir of your honeymoon, have your faces put on a magazine cover at Cashman Photo Magic in Miracle Mile at Planet Hollywood (702 792 3686) or pose with an entertainer on the Strip or downtown.

Films
Honeymooners keen on the movies might find it fun to rent a copy of the 1991 Nicholas Cage comedy *Honeymoon in Vegas*, which is set in the city, to watch on the DVD player in their honeymoon suite.

Directory

Bad Attitude Boutique
953 E. Sahara Ave
• 702 646 9669

Bare Essentials
4029 W. Sahara Ave
• 702 247 4711

General Information
*www.lasvegas.com/
planning-tools/weddings*

Left **Sunset Station Casino sign** Right **Banks of slot machines**

Top 10 Slot Clubs

1 Join Up
If you're planning to gamble, join a slot club. Almost every casino has one, which anyone over the age of 21 can join for free. These clubs give players various rewards in relation to the amount of gambling they do, whether they win or lose.

2 Maximizing Benefits
Compare clubs to determine which one has the prizes you like best and the most advantageous point system. For example, while the number of points required for similar rewards may be the same at two clubs, one of them may award two points for every five dollars that goes through a machine while the other requires only one dollar. You can join as many clubs as you like, but experts advise that you join only one so that you accumulate enough points to earn rewards.

3 Player's Cards
Insert your plastic membership card (issued upon registration) to get your points registered. When accumulated, these points can be exchanged for meals and discounts on rooms (or even free rooms), as well as logo items such as mugs, T-shirts, athletic bags, warm-up jackets, and caps. Some casinos offer cash rewards, too.

4 Slot-club Hosts
Almost every casino employs "slot-club hosts," who circulate around the casino. If you have questions about how to play various machines, ask them; ask, too, how long you have to play the machines to be "comped" for lunch, dinner, or entertainment in the casino's showroom (theater). This is accepted procedure, so don't be shy about asking.

5 Sign-up Savvy
Couples who are in Las Vegas for one trip should sign up together, since they will be issued two cards with points accumulated on the same account. Those who plan more trips to the area, however, will profit by signing up singly: casinos send offers such as a certain number of nights at reduced room rates; by signing up as individuals, the couple may be able to take advantage of twice as many nights at the reduced rate.

6 Payouts
Choose machines with the best payout schedules. These schedules are found on the front of each machine and indicate winning combinations and the value paid out when a combination is hit. As experienced machine players are aware, the video poker and slot machines in any given casino have varying payouts as well as payback ratios (the average percentage the machine pays back to the player).

7 Slot Club Money Management
Remember that in every casino game the house has the advantage (even the 100 percent and better return on the best-paying video poker machines is predicated upon perfect play). Losing $50 to earn a $6.95 buffet award is not a bargain. Add cash to your account and don't bring your wallet to avoid being tempted to spend more than you planned.

8 Table Games
Many casinos include table games in their slot clubs. If you play table games at one of them, contact the pit boss to be sure your playing is included in the point count.

9 Cash-in Advice
Most casinos have both cages and ticket redemption machines so you can cash in any time.

10 Future Plans
If you plan to return to Las Vegas quite soon, begin building gaming loyalty by using certain player's cards and staying at the same hotel.

Left **Slot card** Right **Blackjack table**

10 Gaming Tournaments

1 Tournament Schedules
Gamblers should contact various casinos to determine if any gaming tournaments are planned for the time they will be in Las Vegas. These tournaments range from daily free events and those with low entry fees to four-day tournaments. Blackjack, slot machine, and video poker tourneys are the most popular.

2 Multi-Day Tournaments
Count on a good deal of free time during four-day tournaments, since actual play takes up only two or three hours. Entry fees usually include lodging (or rooms at reduced rates), some meals or food, and beverage credits for the entrant and a guest. Although entry fees may run into the thousands of dollars, typically they're a few hundred dollars. Prize money in the high-stakes tournaments can go as high as a million dollars.

3 Between Rounds
Keep in mind that the casinos' primary reason for putting on tournaments is their belief that participants will gamble in the casino during the time when they're not competing. Most regular slot or video-poker tournaments consist of three rounds of 20–30 minutes each at metered machines and require no money to be spent during tournament play. Winners of each round, as well as the players whose aggregate scores for the three rounds are highest, are awarded prizes.

4 Prizes
The amount of prize money varies, but the majority of tournaments award cash to a large percentage – perhaps a quarter – of the entrants.

5 Blackjack
If blackjack's your game, you'll find that tournaments generally consist of three rounds, with round winners advancing to semi-finals and finals. The entry fee usually covers a certain number of tourney chips, issued at the beginning of the tournament and again before the semi-final and final rounds.

6 High Rollers
If you're a high roller, be sure to get on the invitation list at your casinos of choice. Several casinos don't publicize their tournaments, but instead invite high-end players whose names have been selected from their databases. Complementary accommodations, food, and beverages are generally the properties' finest, and entry fees range all the way from zero to thousands of dollars.

7 Tourney Money Management
For people with finite resources, it is more practical to play in tournaments that have entry fees than those with no fee but participants play with their own money. At tournaments with unlimited buy-ins, players may pay additional money to buy more chips or machine play as the tournament progresses.

8 Playing Plus
When you're competing in a gaming tournament that depends on a combination of luck and skill, stay ahead of the game by sticking to soft drinks and bottled water, rather than complementary alcoholic drinks.

9 Tournament Machines
Don't expect the machines on the casino floor to hit winning combinations as often as the tournament machines. High scores and frequent jackpots create excitement, so as a rule the machines used in tournament play are set to produce lots of action.

10 Repeat Invitations
If you enjoy the gaming tournament experience and want to be invited again, send a thank-you note to the casino's special events director.

Left **Croupier setting a roulette table** Center **Baccarat** Right **Keno**

ᴛᴏᴘ10 Gambling Tips

1 First and Foremost

Remember: gambling is a business. The house almost always wins. Think of it as an evening's entertainment, not as a way of making money. Decide in advance what you are willing to spend, and quit as soon as you have spent it. If you do win anything but want to keep playing then cash in frequently (put your original stake, plus part of your profit, aside) to come out ahead.

2 Casino Games

Blackjack (which is also called "21") is the table game at which players have the best odds. Other popular table games include craps (dice), baccarat, roulette, poker, and three games based on Five Card Stud poker: Caribbean Stud Poker, Let 'er Ride, and Pai Gow.

3 Slot Machines

Many experts believe that slot machines (slots) are addictive. They're the big money-earners for Nevada casinos. Some – video poker, particularly – involve an element of skill. Others are purely games of chance. Newer machines incorporate elements that make them more enticing than the traditional slots.

4 Money Matters

Inserting $10 or $20 bills into slot machine receptors (note that all machines are now coinless) allows for more rapid play, since players need only push a button and the selected amount of coins is deducted. When winning combinations are hit, payouts are added to the total rather than being ejected from the machine. Payouts are by ticket which guests cash at the casino cage.

5 Reading the Payout Tables

Many people who are new to slot machines don't realize that you aren't able to win the highest jackpots posted on a machine unless you insert the maximum number of coins the machine will accept. This means you have to decide whether you want to risk larger amounts, or would prefer to be disappointed if you hit the big one and don't have enough coins in to collect it.

6 Keno

Odds of winning at keno are the lowest of all casino games. The game is based on selecting certain numbers (from 1 to 80) that you hope will be among the 20 numbers to randomly appear. Payouts are based on the number of "catches" (matching numbers selected). Most casinos have keno lounges.

7 Gaming Terms

It is helpful to know at least some of the casino jargon. Hand pay: winnings paid by casino workers rather than machines. Stickman: a casino worker who uses a hook-shaped stick to move dice around a craps table. Shooter: the player whose turn it is to roll the dice. Tokes: tips given for services rendered. RFB comp: complimentary room, food and beverages (usually given to customers who spend a lot). High roller: someone who wagers large amounts. Bust hand in blackjack, a hand that totals more than 21.

8 Gaming Chips

Remember when gambling at the tables that chips are not "play money." At all Las Vegas casinos, $5 chips are red, $25 chips are green and $100 chips are black. The colors of higher denomination chips may vary.

9 Coupon Caution

Take advantage of casino two-for-one or other coupons only if you plan to gamble anyway. Don't let them take advantage of you by enticing you into gambling.

10 Hand Pays

When you hit a jackpot that is paid by casino personnel rather than the machine, it is customary to tip. Any amount is appreciated, but most people tip from three to five percent; big spenders may go as high as 10

For more on casinos and gambling See pp36–7 & 122–3

Left **Laying bets during a craps game** Center **Craps dice** Right **Arizona Charlie's casino**

10 Gambling Risks

1 Forgetting to Take a Break

Don't gamble nonstop. Gambling can be mentally and physically exhausting. If you spend more than an hour deciding whether to hold 'em or fold 'em, or two hours hunched over a slot machine, gamblers' fatigue is bound to set in. Taking a break – perhaps a short stroll outside – will go a long way toward making you feel refreshed.

2 The "It's Due to Hit" Myth

Some gamblers have the idea that since a slot machine hasn't paid any jackpots for a long time, it's due. Not true. Each spin of the reels is an independent event and has nothing to do with what has gone before or will come after.

3 No Good at Math

Beware of penny multiple-coin machines. Casinos make more profit on these machines than on any others. While some machines have nine pay lines, most have 20 or 25. This means that for nine pay lines nine coins must be played if you want to gamble on all the possibilities, or multiples of up to 20 on other machines. As a result, you can bet up to $5 on one push of the deal button.

4 Not Keeping it to Yourself

Don't boast about your winnings anyplace where strangers might hear you. You never know who they might be – con artists or worse.

5 Free Drinks

Resist the cocktail waitresses who circulate throughout the casinos frequently passing out free drinks to gamblers. People who drink excessively don't play as well as they might and have even been known to leave winning tickets behind them when they go.

6 Air Pollution

If you don't like smoking, don't put up with smoke-filled rooms. Some casinos (usually the newer ones) have more effective mechanisms than others for getting rid of smoke. With so many casinos in the city, it isn't hard to find one of them.

7 Cashing Your Paycheck

All sorts of inducements – free drinks, free pulls on slot-machine handles, chances to enter drawings (prize draws) for cars and even houses – are offered so that people will cash their paychecks at casinos.

Why? Because once a paycheck is cashed, it's easier to spend.

8 Neglecting to Set Yourself Limits

Don't neglect to set limits on the amount of money you can afford to lose. Conversely, it's not a good idea to set goals on how much you are going to win before you quit. Probabilities are that it will cost more than the goal itself to reach the goal. It's true that some people do win – at times enormous amounts. But the multi-million and billion-dollar hotel/casinos provide vivid proof that more money is lost than won.

9 Bad Deals

Resist the come-ons some casinos offer of $40 or even $100 in slot play for $20. Play is allowed only on specific machines, and it's only after paying their money that "suckers" learn the real rules.

10 Under-Age Gambling

Don't gamble unless you are 21 years or older. If apprehended, minors are either arrested or given a citation. In either case a court appearance will be required, as the offense is a misdemeanor and subject to penalties that can range from fines to community service or even jail sentences of up to one year.

Left **Excalibur** Center **Learning the ropes** Right **Palace Station**

₁₀ Gaming Lessons

1 Player's Anxiety
To overcome new-player jitters, it's wise to take lessons in the games you want to play. These are usually available at the casinos listed Monday through Friday: they last about an hour and are free.

2 House Rules
Even if you play poker or baccarat regularly with friends, the benefit of lessons is that you will learn the procedures and protocols of casino play. Not knowing the rules can be embarrassing.

3 Timing
You'll get more out of gaming lessons if you take them in the morning. Casinos – the setting for most lessons – tend to be much noisier and distracting as the day wears on, which can make it difficult to concentrate on what the instructor is saying.

4 Tipping
Although there is no charge for the classes, your instructor will appreciate a tip. Any amount between $2 and $5 would be appropriate.

MGM Grand

5 A Winner
More than a half-dozen casinos on the Strip offer free gaming lessons. Among them are Excalibur, Circus Circus, Tropicana, and Imperial Palace. Class hours and the games taught vary from casino to casino.

6 Exotic Games
When you're ready to tackle Pai Gow, Caribbean Stud, and Let it Ride poker, phone Golden Nugget or Planet Hollywood for their lesson times.

7 Downtown Lessons
If you want to keep away from the Strip, then Golden Nugget is one of the few downtown casinos that offers gaming lessons.

8 Off-Strip Instruction
Further afield – and a good choice if you have a car and don't want any parking hassles – Gold Coast Hotel and Casino is reputed to have good gaming instruction.

9 TV Classes
Instead of participating in group gaming lessons, guests at several hotels can learn how to play most casino games by watching the in-house programs on the TV sets in their rooms. Programs repeat at regular intervals throughout the day.

10 A Cautionary Note
So you've taken lessons. That doesn't mean you're an expert yet! Watch actual play before you start wagering, and then bet minimum amounts until you're experienced at casino play.

Blackjack

Directory of Casinos Offering Gaming Lessons

Caesars Palace
3500 Las Vegas Blvd S.
• 800 364 6001

Excalibur
3850 Las Vegas Blvd S.
• 702 597 7777

Gold Coast Hotel & Casino
4000 W. Flamingo Rd
• 702 367 7111

Golden Nugget
129 Fremont St
• 702 385 7111

Planet Hollywood
3667 Las Vegas Blvd S.
• 866 919 7472

Tropicana Las Vegas
3801 Las Vegas Blvd S.
• 800 462 8767

Streetsmart

On Levels 2-7
Near Elevators

Left **Wheelchair-access sign** Right **Monorail**

TOP 10 Las Vegas for Disabled Visitors

1 ADA Coordinators
Las Vegas is perhaps the world's most accessible city for people with disabilities. If you have any questions or any particular needs, have your travel agent contact the hotel's Americans with Disabilities Act (ADA) coordinator prior to your visit. Every major hotel-casino has one, responsible for ensuring that the facilities are accessible.

2 Airport Shuttles
Airport shuttles equipped with lifts are available at the airport baggage-claim area doors 1, 3, and 4. You may have to phone for a lift-equipped taxi, but direct-line phones are located in the baggage-claim area. Find out if car-rental company shuttles to their lots are lift-equipped, and let them know in advance if you need rear van seats removed and a ramp.

3 ADA Requirements
Bellagio, The Mirage, and Imperial Palace have the reputation of being the best equipped for people with disabilities. All hotels, however, are supposed to have some rooms especially equipped for disabled guests. You may have to hunt around to find such specific amenities as roll-in showers, assisted-listening devices, vibrating alarm clocks, or televisions with telecaption devices.

4 Casino Accessibility
Every casino has accessible slot machines, and many have lowered tables with wheelchair access. Most bingo parlors have Braille and large-print game cards, and many casinos, if asked in advance, provide sign-language interpreters for gaming lessons.

5 Swimming Pools
Most hotels have lifts to assist guests into swimming pools; some of the pools with sand beaches also have wheelchair-accessible beach entrances.

6 Showroom Space
All Las Vegas venues for production and other shows (generally referred to as showrooms) have special areas for wheelchairs. Let personnel know in advance, since wheelchair users are often seated first.

7 Ramps and Restrooms
You can expect all public buildings, attractions, and hotel-casinos to be ramped and to have restrooms for the disabled. Curbs on most streets have been modified so that they are wheelchair accessible. City buses are fully accessible, as are some taxis, trams, shuttles, and the

monorail. It is also possible to rent motorized carts (mechanized one-passenger carts used in lieu of wheelchairs).

8 Medication Schedules
If you need to take medication at certain times, wear a watch – there are no clocks in casinos.

9 Pedestrian Overcrossings
Don't worry about having to climb stairs at overhead pedestrian crossings. They can be reached by elevators or escalators.

10 Information
ADA coordinators may be able to answer your queries. Try the website listed below, too.

Directory

www.lasvegas.com

Bellagio

Left **Gay bookstore** Right **The city at night**

ᴛᴏᴘ10 Gay and Lesbian Visitors

Acceptance
Opinions vary as to the degree of acceptance of gays and lesbians in Las Vegas. While the city is outwardly liberal and permissive – camp, even – its straight citizens are considered by some to be ultra-conservative in their views. Having said that, the city elected its first openly gay representative to the State Assembly in 1996. Many Las Vegas businesses, too, allow for what is euphemistically described as a "domestic partner" in their health insurance plans. For the most part, locals welcome everyone and open hostility is incredibly rare.

Gay Organizations
There are more than 75 gay organizations active in Las Vegas, representing all sorts of interests, from singing to motor-cycling. Though not exclusively geared towards the LBGTQ population, the Erotic Heritage Museum has a full calendar of educational workshops and lectures in a comfortable environment.

Where the Action Is
The main gay section of Las Vegas, containing a number of gay bars and clubs, is in the Paradise Road, Harmon, and Tropicana avenues area, just east of the MGM Grand, called the Fruit Loop.

Clubs
The well-known nightclub Krave has been around for a while and is located on the Las Vegas Strip. Charlie's, Piranha Nightclub, and Share Nightclub are also gaining a loyal following. For something more low-key, try Free Zone.

Transgender Bar
The Las Vegas Lounge is one of the city's most popular transgender bars.

Internet Information
You can get information about gay and lesbian venues in the city from several websites. Try www.lasvegas.com for listings of accommodations and restaurants that are gay-owned or gay-friendly.

Meeting Venue
The Gay & Lesbian Community Center of Southern Nevada (known also just as The Center, *below*) sponsors frequent social events and is a venue for meetings of various LGBTQ groups. It also offers free and confidential tests for HIV on Monday and Thursday. Timings vary.

Reading Material
Get Booked, the city's small but well-stocked gay bookstore, is open seven days a week.

Publications
For local gay-related news, pick up a copy of *QVegas*. You can find it around town, subscribe to the online newsletter, or browse the website.

Help Line
The organization PFLAG (Parents and Friends of Lesbians and Gays) runs a help line offering information and resources, listed below.

Left **Bank of America sign** Center **ATM machine** Right **$50 bill**

⑩ Banking

1 Vegas Banking Hours

Most banks are open from 9am to either 5 or 6pm Monday through Friday, and 9am–1pm on Saturday. Branches located in supermarkets tend to have longer hours and stay open all day on Saturday and sometimes on Sunday afternoon.

2 ATMs

Using ATMs for cash and credit cards for purchases usually ensures the best exchange rates for foreign visitors. Be prepared to pay a fee, which will be charged to your account, for using an ATM at a bank that is not your own. Instructions for use should appear in English and Spanish, and sometimes Japanese.

3 Drive-Through Banking

For many simple money transactions, drive-through banking (often spelled "drive-thru" on signs) is the most convenient method. The windows are usually open for an additional half-hour at the beginning and end of the bank's regular business day. Drive-throughs usually have cash machines (ATMs), too.

4 Getting Hold of Cash

Check-cashing services, located at various places along the Strip and downtown, charge large fees, so it's best to try to use alternative methods of getting cash. Cash advances on credit cards are available from cash-advance machines at all hotel-casinos, but again the service will cost you: the typical fee is 5 percent (that's a $50 fee for cashing $1,000), with larger percentages for smaller amounts.

5 Cashing Personal Checks at Hotels

Most hotels will cash guests' personal checks, provided they are in US dollars. It is not general policy, however, to cash checks for non-guests.

6 Foreign Currency

Unlike banks in Europe, only a few Las Vegas banks handle foreign currency. Most convenient of these is probably Bank of America. Many hotel-casinos will exchange foreign currency from major countries, but they charge a fee in addition to the hotel's own exchange rate.

7 Traveler's Checks

Traveler's checks can be cashed at any bank or hotel-casino. Try to get the checks in US dollars to avoid paying an exchange fee each time you cash one; if you do use checks in a foreign currency, try to get large denominations to save on fees when you cash the checks.

8 Credit Cards

All major credit cards are accepted at most businesses in Las Vegas.

9 Dollar Bills

If you are unfamiliar with US banknotes, take heed of the fact that they are notoriously hard to differentiate; pay special attention to this when handing over money to taxi drivers etc. A $1 "bill" is just the same size and color as a $20. Denominations start at $1 and run as high as $100.

10 Small Change

The US dollar (sometimes referred to as a "buck") is divided into 100 cents (called pennies). Coins come in one cent, five cent (nickel), ten cent (dime), 25 cent (quarter), and 50 cent (half-dollar) denominations.

Directory

Bank of America
4795 S. Maryland Pkwy • 702 654 4120 • Open 9am–5pm Mon–Thu, 9am–6pm Fri, 9am–1pm Sat • www.bankofamerica.com

Left **Public Internet access** Center **Postage stamp** Right **Post Office sign**

TOP 10 Communications

1 Publications for Visitors

Useful entertainment guides include *What's On*, *Where*, and *Monorail Magazine*. Look out for the discount coupons for meals or shows.

2 Las Vegas Newspapers

The city's principal newspaper, the *Las Vegas Review-Journal* is published daily. The most widely read alternative newspapers are *Las Vegas Weekly*, and *Vegas Seven*, both free and published weekly.

3 Internet Access

Most hotels include Internet access in the resort fee. If you require public Internet access, visit a local print shop such as FedEx Office, which provides computer usage for a fee and free Wi-Fi. Public libraries also offer free Internet services, and you can access free Wi-Fi at independent locations of coffeeshops such as Starbucks and Coffee Bean & Tea Leaf, as well as at branches of McDonald's.

Public phone

4 Making Calls

To place a call within Las Vegas and environs, omit the 702 area code. When telephoning outside the area, you will need to dial a 1, followed by the appropriate area code and seven-digit number. Local calls are usually free from hotel rooms. The easiest way to pay for long-distance calls is to insert your credit card. As elsewhere in the world, long-distance calls made from hotel rooms cost a great deal more than those made from pay phones.

5 Public Telephones

You'll find public telephones, or pay phones, outside supermarkets and gas stations, and in restaurants, hotels, and casinos all around the area. When they're inside buildings, phones are usually located near the restrooms.

6 Cell Phones

It is difficult to get cell phone service on the Strip and in the casinos. Calling or texting from an open space is often more successful.

7 Hotel Business Centers

Most major hotels have business centers for guests' use (although not for free) equipped with the latest computers; some also offer secretarial services and have guest rooms equipped with "dataports" for computers, fax, and internet usage.

8 Western Union

If you need to send international telegrams, ask hotel personnel where to find the nearest Western Union office. You can also use Western Union for wiring funds.

9 Post Offices

You can have incoming mail sent either direct to your hotel or to "General Delivery" at any US Post Office in the city. The post office that is conveniently located for most visitors is the one downtown, though many pharmacies and banks sell stamps.

10 TV and Radio

Choose from numerous local radio and TV stations. If the local fare fails to satisfy, your hotel is very likely to have cable or satellite TV.

Directory

FedEx Office
4750 W. Sahara Ave
• 702 870 7011

US Post Office
201 Las Vegas Blvd S.
• 702 382 5779

1801 S. Decatur Blvd
• 702 220 8454

 For more sources of information See p115

Left **Security guard** Right **Police car**

Top 10 Things to Avoid

Traffic Tangle
1 Any street intersecting with Las Vegas Boulevard South means slow traffic, but if possible use the streets that run parallel to the Strip, such as Industrial Rd on the west and Koval Ln on the east. Allow yourself extra time during rush hour.

Crime Zone
2 Although the Strip and the five-block Fremont Street Experience pedestrian mall are considered safe at any time, certain areas in North Las Vegas and on S. Maryland Parkway, around Sunrise Hospital, are not. The area north of Las Vegas library on Las Vegas Boulevard North is perhaps the roughest neighborhood in town. Use caution when visiting.

Con Artists
3 Rings of confidence tricksters – men and women – frequently operate in Nevada, with all sorts of scams. They prey primarily, but not exclusively, on the elderly. Beware anyone who approaches you with an offer that seems too good to be true, and never agree to collect jackpot winnings for another person on the promise that you'll be paid for doing so. Card sharps in particular look for suckers. Don't be one: if a deals sounds too good to be true, it probably is.

Prostitution
4 Prostitution is legal in the state of Nevada except in five counties, including Clark County. Las Vegas is in Clark County, so apprehended prostitutes and their customers are subject to fines and imprisonment. Bear in mind that strip clubs in the downtown and Strip area are legitimate businesses and not brothels.

Cache Your Cash
5 Don't wear expensive jewelry: it alerts robbers or pickpockets to the fact that you would be a lucrative target. Keep valuables in your room safe if there is one, or in the hotel's safe if there isn't. Keep your belongings with you at all times: the excitement of the bright lights, music, and carnival atmosphere can be distracting. If you win a large amount of money, ask for it in the form of a check rather than cash. Casinos will also provide security escorts for customers who request them.

Don't Let the Kids Roam
6 Do not allow youngsters under the age of 16 to go out on their own; children under 12 should not go without adults to malls or game arcades, even if they are in a group.

Car Trouble
7 Avoid poorly lighted garages and parking lots at night, especially when they seem deserted. Lock your car doors even when you are driving. Put all packages and luggage in the trunk. When you leave your car at valet parking, it's wise to remove anything of value and have only your car and trunk keys on the key-ring.

Mealtime Precautions
8 Cold soup and warm potato salad are potential sources of food poisoning, so when eating at buffets always make sure that the food that is supposed to be hot is hot, and the food that is supposed to be cold is cold. The best options are those that are freshly prepared on request, such as omelets and pasta.

Panhandlers
9 It's up to you, of course, whether you give money to panhandlers (beggars), but you might consider contributing instead to charities that provide food and shelter for the homeless.

Law-Enforcement Officers
10 Despite the carefree atmosphere of Las Vegas, the police department is strict about enforcing the city's laws. Don't do anything here that you wouldn't do in your own home town and you should be ok.

For advice about traveling through the desert **See p133**

Left **Desert sign** Center **Temperature gauge** Right **Drugstore sign**

🔟 Ways to Stay Healthy

1 Becoming Acclimated
Give your body a chance to become acclimated upon arrival before engaging in strenuous activity, especially if you have traveled a long distance or from a much different climate or altitude. Because of the dry weather, for example, people prone to nosebleeds may experience problems.

2 Taking the Water
Nevada's low humidity means that you must drink plenty of fluids each day (alcoholic beverages don't count), especially during the summer. Dehydration and heat stroke account for many emergency medical service calls.

3 Solar Protection
Slather on the sunscreen whenever you go outdoors, not just when at the hotel pool. Even when the Nevada sunlight is filtered through clouds, it can burn.

4 Pollution
Pollution caused by blowing desert dust, vehicle emissions, and microscopic grit from construction sites can be a problem for people with respiratory problems – keep medication to hand.

5 Allergies and Arthritis
People with allergies to dust and sagebrush may have a problem in Las Vegas. However, most people with arthritis find that the low humidity is more comfortable for them than climates with higher humidity.

6 Overindulgence
Drinking too much is easy in the casinos' party atmosphere of bright lights and free drinks. It's up to you how much you indulge, but do not even think about driving afterward. Under Nevada law, the blood alcohol level at which a person is presumed intoxicated is 0.08 percent and can bring about a court appearance and heavy fine if the driver is stopped by police. In the case of an accident involving fatalities, it can result in imprisonment.

7 Insurance
Travel insurance may not be mandatory for visitors to the USA, but it is emphatically recommended because emergency medical and dental care can be extremely expensive. In most cases, people incurring medical expenses are required to make payment (or arrangement for it) before leaving the clinic, hospital, or physician's office.

8 Take Your Medicine
Remember that there are no clocks in casinos: the excitement of gaming may make you forget to take your regular medications. (Also be aware of those that shouldn't be taken with alcohol.) To have prescriptions filled, go either to drugstores (pharmacies) or the pharmacy departments of supermarkets, several of which are open 24 hours.

9 In Case of Illness
Since Las Vegas has more tourists than any other US destination, the medical professional is especially mindful of the need for in-room service (not usual in the USA). If you develop a condition that requires medical attention, Inn-House Doctor, Inc. offers 24/7 consultations and the doctors make hotel visits if necessary. Harmon Medical Center offers a walk-in clinic, open from 8am–8pm Monday–Friday; you will need medical insurance and some ID to use this service. There are several emergency rooms in Las Vegas if needed.

10 Medical Emergencies
In case of an extreme medical emergency, dial 911 from any telephone (remember to dial the appropriate number to get an outside line if you're in your hotel room) or dial "O" and ask the operator to dial it for you and send help to your room immediately.

Above **A desert walk just after sunrise, before ground temperatures rise**

⁑10 Desert Precautions

1 Water Requirements
Be sure to carry drinking water. A gallon per person per day is suggested. The outdoor enthusiasts' greatest dangers are from hypothermia (extreme over-cooling) and heat-stroke (extreme overheating). Preventing dehydration helps avoid the latter. Carry water for your car, too. Even the radiators of new cars can overheat when outside temperatures hit 120°F (nearly 50°C).

2 Car Check
Be sure your car is in good mechanical condition and that it has a full gas tank. Stay on paved roads; do not drive on the shoulder, if possible, because there is danger of being trapped in the sand.

3 Flash Floods
Don't try to drive through flooded areas. If water begins to rise over the road, it is actually best to abandon your car and move to high ground.

4 Don't Go Solo
Never venture into the desert alone, and don't go hiking without a map and a good compass, even if you have a Global Positioning System (GPS).

5 Tell Somebody
Whenever you go hiking in the desert, advise a park ranger or other responsible person of your destination and estimated time of return. In case you become lost, search and rescue teams can work more effectively if they have information to guide them.

6 Dress Properly
Layered clothing slows dehydration and minimizes exposure. Summer temperatures well above 100°F (38°C) are not uncommon, and winter temperatures can plunge below freezing. During the course of a typical day and night, there may be a huge variation in temperature.

7 Be Prepared
Always carry a first-aid kit when hiking. Every hiker over the age of 12 should know CPR and basic first aid.

8 Dangerous Creatures
Beware of rattlesnakes and scorpions. Before you go, learn how to treat their bites (getting medical help as quickly as possible is recommended). Other dangerous animals and insects that live in the desert are gila monsters, mountain lions, wild boar, bears, killer bees, and centipedes. Wildlife may seem tame but will attack if they feel threatened or that their young are in danger.

9 Cover Your Head
Wear a hat to help prevent heatstroke whenever you are subjected to the desert sun's rays in the middle of the day – even when it is overcast. Even if you spend only minutes outside, you should protect your skin with sunscreen and use lip balm. Moisturizer is helpful in the desert climate as well.

10 Curb Your Curiosity
Stay away from abandoned mines. They are very dangerous because of the possibility of cave-ins, sharp drop-offs, and deadly gases.

Directory

Emergency Number
911

Inn-House Doctor, Inc
702 259 1616

Harmon Medical Center
*150 E. Harmon Ave
• Map Q3 • 702 796 1116*

24 Hour Vegas Hotel Doctor
702 677 2644

133

Left **Wigwam** Center **RV Parking lot entrance, Laughlin** Right **Tent in a national park**

Camping and Houseboating

1 Research your Campsites

Camping in city parks is generally not permitted. Camping in state and national parks is permitted in spaces designated for that use, and some off-trail overnight camping for hikers is allowed. Most state and national park and recreation area campgrounds have a first come, first served policy, so arrive early to have a better chance of getting a site. However, since other campgrounds require reservations, you'll need to contact them in advance. Be sure to obey all campground rules regarding fires, keeping pets on a leash, and the disposal of trash.

2 Tent Sites

There are only a few tent sites at Red Rock Canyon but if you are lucky enough to find one free you can stay up to 14 days. There are also tent sites at Mt. Charleston and campsites around Lake Mead.

3 Reservations

Make reservations at privately owned campgrounds as far in advance as possible. As camping increases in popularity, it is more difficult to get a space without reservations. This is especially true during the summer when schoolchildren are on vacation and in the early autumn, a favorite holiday time for seniors.

4 Casino Campgrounds

It's especially important to reserve early if you want to stay at one of the casino camping facilities. Las Vegas KOA is adjacent to Circus Circus on the Strip, and Sam's Town RV Park is near Sam's Town Hotel & Gambling Hall.

5 RV-Friendly Parking Lots

Laughlin is the most RV-friendly area in southern Nevada. Recreational vehicles can be parked in its casino parking lots overnight and there are several recreational vehicle parks on the other side of the Colorado River in Bullhead City, Arizona.

6 RV Rentals

If you would like to rent a recreational vehicle while you're in Las Vegas, you can choose from more than half a dozen rental companies. You will find them listed in the yellow pages of the Las Vegas telephone directory and on the Internet.

7 Campground Caution

Never camp in or near a dry wash (the course water takes when it rains) because of the potential for flash floods. Do not camp on the top of a large hill because of the danger from lightning and extreme winds.

8 Downpours

If you are camping in the desert when heavy rains begin, move to high ground immediately – at least 30 to 40 ft (10 m) above the canyon floor or bottom of a dry wash is recommended.

9 Houseboating

To rent a houseboat, contact either Seven Crown Resorts or Forever Resorts well in advance. The Forever Resorts marina at Callville Bay, the closer of the two, is about a 45-minute drive from the Las Vegas Strip.

10 Season Selection

Summer may be unpleasantly hot but is the peak season for campers and houseboaters: make arrangements up to a year in advance. The best rental values are during the winter, but the weather may not be pleasant. Consider renting a houseboat either during spring or fall.

Directory

Las Vegas KOA
500 Circus Circus Drive
• *702 733 9707*

Sam's Town RV Park
5225 Boulder Highway
• *702 456 7777*

Seven Crown Resorts
800 752 9669 • www. sevencrown.com

Forever Resorts
800 255 5561

Left **Mule riding** Center **Luxury hotel interior** Right **New Year celebrations, the Strip**

TOP 10 Tips on Booking a Hotel

1 Choose an Appropiate Hotel

Take your personal travel style into consideration when choosing where to stay. If you like action and don't mind noise, you will want to stay on the Strip or downtown. If gaming will play only a minor part in your holiday, you will be better off staying at accommodations that don't have a casino.

2 Travel Agents

The easiest way to reserve Las Vegas rooms is by having a travel agent book them for you. However, travel agents often do not have access to money-saving resources or time to access them.

3 Arrangements on the Internet

Almost all major Las Vegas hotel/casinos have their own websites on which they offer online bookings and advertise promotions. These are listed under their main entries within this book.

4 Packages

Explore the many airline/ accommodations packages. The least expensive of these are gambling junkets that usually include airline flights and two- to four-night hotel stays, based on double occupancy. There are often, but not always, several hotel choices in various price categories.

5 Individual Requirements

To make the most satis-factory room arrange-ments, phone the hotel directly to talk with a reservationist. By dis-cussing your needs with a person who knows the hotel intimately you are more likely to get exactly the room that you want.

6 Bargains

For rock-bottom Las Vegas room rates, time your stay to coincide with the days preceding and following New Year's Eve and New Year's Day (or the entire weekend if New Year falls within one), as well as the days between the National Finals Rodeo and Christ-mas. Hotel websites are usually the best places to find special deals throughout the year.

7 Times to Avoid

Room rates are usual-ly higher over weekends and holidays, and can more than quadruple when there is a major convention at the hotel or nearby *(see p117)*.

8 National Parks

National parks in the USA are extremely popular – especially those in the American Southwest. The effect of this is that booking accommodations within the parks, as well as whitewater rafting and mule rides at the Grand Canyon should be made at least a year in advance. Otherwise, you will have to stay in an outlying area.

9 Outlying Areas

Accommodations in Laughlin, Boulder City, Mesquite, and areas within the Las Vegas orbit are not as difficult to obtain nor as expensive as most of those in Las Vegas or Henderson. Bear in mind that you will need a car to access them easily.

10 Last-Minute Rates

If you are extremely flexible, you can take advantage of last-minute travel packages available through most travel booking companies, which can be good value.

Houseboats in the Seven Crown Resort

Index

Index

Acknowledgments

The Author

Connie Emerson, who has lived in Nevada for more than 30 years, writes travel articles for national and international publications.

Produced by Blue Island Publishing, Highbury, London

Editorial Director
Rosalyn Thiro
Art Director
Stephen Bere
Editors
Michael Ellis, Charlotte Rundall
Designers
Tony Foo, Ian Midson
Picture Research
Ellen Root
Research Assistance
Amaia Allende, Emma Wilson
Main Photographer
Demetrio Carrasco
Other Photographers
Nigel Hicks, Alan Keohane, Tim Ridley, Greg Ward
Artwork
Chris Orr & Associates
Proofreader
Stephanie Driver
Index
Hilary Bird

AT DORLING KINDERSLEY:

Director of Publishing
Gillian Allan
Senior Publishing Manager
Louise Bostock Lang
Publishing Manager
Kate Poole
Senior Art Editor
Marisa Renzullo
Cartography Co-ordinator
Casper Morris
DTP
Jason Little
Production
Sarah Dodd, Marie Ingledew
Cartography
John Plumer

Revisions Team

Ashwin Raju Adimari, Tora Agarwala, Emma Anacootee, Claire Baranowski, Bob Barnes, Marta Bescos, Louise Cleghorn, Karen Constanti, Connie Emerson, Mariana Evmolpidou, Anna Freiberger, Rhiannon Furbear, Jo Gardner, Camilla Gersh, Eric Grossman, JoAnna Haugen, Rebecca Ingram Frisch, Claire Jones, Bharti Karakoti, Maite Lantaron, Sam Merrell, Marianne Petrou, Collette Sadler, AnneLise Sorensen, Avantika Sukhia, Ajay Verma, Karen Villabona, Ros Walford, Alex Whittleton

Dorling Kindersley would like to thank all the hotels, restaurants, shops, museums, galleries, and other sights for their assistance and kind permission to photograph at their establishments.

Placement Key: t = top; tl–top left; tr–top right; c–center; cb–center below; b–bottom; bl–bottom left; br–bottom right; l–left; d–detail.

ALAMY IMAGES: Lynn Sutherland 82tr. THE BARRICK MUSEUM AT UNLV: 44b; Courtesy of THE BELLAGIO: Russell MacMasters Photography 2tl, 14b, 15c, 31br, 46b, 50c, 77c, 120tl; BINION'S: 13bc; THE BLUE MAN GROUP: Ken Howard 38tr; BOUL- DER DAM BREWING CO: 96tc, m; BUREAU OF RECLAMATION: Andrew Pernick 6cl, 10–11c, 92t.
CAESARS ENTERTAINMENT: 71br; Courtesy of CAESARS PALACE: 64tr; 74tl, 76tr; PURE nightclub 42tr; CHINOIS: 47ca; CIRQUE DU SOLEIL INC: Jeremy Daniel & Richard Turmine 29tl; photos by Tomas Muscionico Costumes Marie-Chantale Vaillancourt 38tc, 119tr, Photo Veronique Vial Costumes

Acknowledgments

Dominique Lemieux 38c, 119c; © Al Seib 38b; CORBIS: Bettmann 30c, 31t, 120tr; Richard Cummins 50tr; Terra/Rudy Sulgan 8–9c. DREAMSTIME.COM: Walter Arce 86tr.

Courtesy THE DESERT INN: 135tc. EMERGENCY ARTS: 13tr; Courtesy of EXCALIBUR: 135tr. FASHION SHOW: 52tr; courtesy of THE FORUM SHOPS: 26t, 26b; THE FUNK HOUSE LAS VEGAS: 83tr. Courtesy of GET BOOKED: 128tl; GOLDEN NUGGET Las Vegas: 97tc. HARD ROCK CAFE Las Vegas: 90tc; HARD ROCK HOTEL: Erik Kabik 42bl; Courtesy of HARRAH'S: 36tr; HULTON ARCHIVE: Archive Pictures 30tc. Courtesy of JUBILEE: 3tcl, 39t, 119tl; JW MARRIOTT LAS VEGAS RESORT & SPA: 36tl, 88tl. LAS VEGAS CONVENTION & VISITORS AUTHORITY: 56tl, 66cla; LAS VEGAS MAGAZINE: 115cb; LAS VEGAS MINI GRAN PRIX: 75tc; LAS VEGAS NEWS BUREAU: 6tl, 6bl, 7br, 7crb, 8, 8bc, 12cla, 12–13bl, 24–25c, 28cla, 28crb, 28–29c, 29cra, 80t, 82tl, 114tl, 115tl; LAS VEGAS SUN: Lori Cain 58tr; Steve Marcus 58b; Aaron Mayes 85, 87tr; Sam Morris 59t, 86b; Ethan Miller 84tr, 87cb; Marsh Starks 58tl, 59b; LEONARDO MEDIA LTD.: 28bc, 96bc. Courtesy of MAND- ALAY BAY: 112tr; MANDARIN ORI- ENTAL: 29bl;

courtesy of the MGM GRAND: 46tc 126b, 128tr; MGM RESORTS INTERNATIONAL: 46cla; MGM MIRAGE: 36cb, 42tc, 47tr, 52br, 64bl 65tr, 77tr, 117tr, 118tc, 118tl, 118tr; courtesy of THE MIRAGE 46tc, 64tl, 66b, 73b, 117tr.

N9NEGROUP: 42c; NHPA: David Middleton 104c.

PHOTOFM.COM: Fred Morledge 57cl; PLAZA HOTEL & CASINO: 46tl THE RAINBOW COMPANY YOUTH THEATER: Tom Dyer 66tr; RIO SUITE HOTEL: 87bl.

THE SMITH CENTER: 40tr; STATION CASINOS: 67tr, 75tl; STONE: Kerrick James 110–11; courtesy of STRATOSPHERE TOWER: 56b. TAO: Al Powers 42tl; Courtesy of TI 76tl; TOWN SQUARE LAS VEGAS: 53c; TRYST: 43tl. Courtesy of THE VENETIAN: 20t, 32tl, 71t. WOLFGANG PUCK'S SPAGO: Jeffrey Green 27bc. Courtesy of WYNN LAS VEGAS: 51br, Scott Forest 23tr, Robert Miller 7c, 22cla, 22–23, 23cr, Tomasz Rossa 22bc, 38tl, 119tr. Pull out map cover – DK IMAGES: Rough Guides/Demetrio Carrasco. Front endpapers – BINION'S: bc.

All other images are © Dorling Kindersley. For further information see *www.dkimages.com*